My Journey in Karate

My Journey in Karate
The Sabaki Way

Kancho Joko Ninomiya
with Ed Zorensky

Frog, Ltd.
Berkeley, California

My Journey in Karate, The Sabaki Way

Copyright © 2000 by Kancho Joko Ninomiya with Ed Zorensky.
No portion of this book, except for brief review, may be reproduced
in any form without written permission of the publisher.
For information, contact Frog Ltd. c/o North Atlantic Books.

Published by Frog, Ltd.
Frog, Ltd. Books are distributed by North Atlantic Books
P.O. Box 12327
Berkeley, California 94712

Cover Photo by Ed and Nancy Zorensky
Cover design by Ed Zorensky
Book design by Jan Camp

Printed in the United States of America by Malloy Lithographing

Library of Congress Cataloging-in-Publication Data

Ninomiya, Kancho Joko

My journey in karate, the sabaki way / Kancho Joko Ninomiya,
with Ed Zorensky

Library of Congress Catalog-in-Publication Data

Ninomiya, Kancho Joko.
    My journey in karate: the sabaki way / by Kancho Joko Ninomiya with Ed Zorensky.
        p. cm.
    Originally published: Boston : Knightsbridge Pub. Co., 1991.
    ISBN 1-58394-017-0 (alk. paper)
        1. Ninomiya, Kancho Joko. 2. Martial artists–Japan–Biography. I. Zorensky, Ed,
1948- II. Title.

GV1113.N56 A3 2000
796.815'3'092–dc21
[B]

99-087452

1 2 3 4 5 6 7 8 9 / 03 02 01 00

To all of my students . . .
and especially to those who have been with me
over the years:

Joel Humphrey, Don Doubleday, Dave and Dan Fisher,
Randy Randall, Vernon Owens, Paul O'Malley, Frank Keyes,
Ed and Nancy Zorensky, Brett Layser, Ralph Rhoads,
Nobuhiko Kishi, Greg Vahenian, Humberto Leon, Dan Lockhart,
Toshi Isogai, Yukihiro Izawa, Masuda Koji, Yasuhiko Nakano,
Noboru Hino, Shingo Asayama, Paden Wolfe,
Yuji and Beth Iwakura, Yoshi and Jane Ota, and Kenji Nogi.

Your support and your example
have helped make this journey possible.

Osu.

Contents

Chapter Six (continued)

Acknowledgements

I would like to thank Yoshi and Jane Ota for helping to translate my conversation with Sensei Nobuyuki Kishi from the Japanese.

Thanks also to Mr. Esao Hashimoto for working with Ed Zorensky and myself in editing the various drafts of the first edition of this book. Hashimoto has been a wildlife technician with the Colorado Division of Wildlife and has published articles on wildlife in Japanese magazines. He lives in Denver, where he is now a successful businessman, and has shared with me the dream of working and living in America.

Finally, I would like to express my gratitude to Ed Zorensky with whom I spent many hours recounting my past and shaping this story. A former teacher, Ed has worked in politics, television, and public radio, and has published articles and short stories in various publications. In addition to helping produce Sabaki technique and tournament videotapes, Ed designed, illustrated, and helped me to write *The Sabaki Method* technique book. He is a *yondan* training at the headquarters in Denver. He and his wife Nancy ran the southeast Denver dojo for eleven years.

Preface

Sunlight flooded the large practice room of our school, reflecting from the mirrors at the far end of the floor. It was a warm September afternoon, the sky a deep blue that you find only in the Rocky Mountains. I was alone in the *dojo*, sitting by the windows and reading through the roll of students, checking off names of those who were ready for the next promotion test.

I sensed the stranger before I even heard his feet shuffling just outside the open door. He looked to be about 6 feet 6 inches tall, 240 pounds or so, built like a football linebacker. He was standing at the window, pretending to examine a poster, but I could feel his eyes measuring me in a way that made the hair stand up on the back of my neck. He strolled the length of the window and back again. Finally he stepped inside the door.

"Can I help you?" I asked.

He didn't answer. He let his eyes gaze at the bulletin board. After a moment he strolled over to my desk.

"Are you the champion from Japan?" he asked.

A bus roared by, its brakes hissing as it stopped in the next block. I looked him over without answering. He was dressed in jeans and a white T-shirt. He wore a brown, flat cap and carried a gym bag slung over one shoulder.

"Are you Joko Ninomiya?" he demanded.

"Yes," I said. "What can I do for you?"

His brown hair stuck out under the greasy cap. He narrowed his eyes and tilted his head back. "I've trained in three different styles," he said self-importantly. He had a cocky way of standing with his weight on one leg, his thumbs hooked in the pockets of his jeans. "I'd like to spar with you."

There are so many parts of our Japanese tradition that Americans don't understand. They have seen movies and read the stories about fighters from one school coming to challenge the leader of another school. They see the outside of our tradition, the surface, but only those who have committed to the martial arts—those who have gone beyond black belts to the higher levels of understanding—know what that tradition means. It means that if you have chosen karate as your way, then you are ready to give up your life if you are challenged. It is a way of living on the edge of existence, at death's door. It means submitting to the possibility of death and accepting it at any moment that it may appear.

I have never taken challenges lightly. I needed to make sure that this scruffy fellow standing in my dojo with an arrogant challenge burning in his eyes knew exactly the stakes at hand. I closed the roll book. I laid the pen on the desk.

"If you mean you want to practice, to just spar," I said, "no thanks."

"What do you mean, 'no thanks?' I thought you were a champion," he said. "I want to fight you!"

"Are you challenging me? Because if you just want to practice, I'm not interested. But if you're challenging me, I'll fight you. You understand the difference?"

He weighed my words, and then nodded. "Yeah, let's fight."

"All right," I said.

I stepped out from behind the desk. I nodded to the dressing room at the back of the dojo. He started across the carpet. "Please leave your shoes at the door," I reminded him.

He grunted, kicked off his shoes, and started to the back of the dojo. My mind was focused on one thought only: I would have to knock down this cocky stranger and make him stay down. I remembered the lesson I had learned early on from Hideyuki Ashihara, my first and only karate teacher, and later on the kancho, or leader, of Ashihara Karate. When I was still in high school, a challenger showed up at the dojo in Yawatahama, and we fought. I handled him well, but when he finally gave up he was still on his feet. Kancho Ashihara shook his head and said, "Your heart is too nice. You must knock him down. Otherwise, he will change his story and say it was a draw."

I did what I was told that day. And I have done so ever since. The importance of honor is a very difficult thing for most Westerners to understand. Honor has no weight, no size or color. Its value is gauged only by the heart and spirit. What Kancho had taught me that day in the dojo was the importance and seriousness of a challenge. I didn't know whether my opponent understood the seriousness of his challenge. If he did not, I was willing to teach him—with my life, if necessary.

I don't mean to sound melodramatic. I am simply talking about the way I live my life, a life that has been spent in *karate-do* (the "way" of karate). The Japanese word *do* means "way" or "path." In this sense, karate-do is more than physical conditioning or the mastery of a few self-defense techniques. It is a lifelong journey in pursuit of an art form and all the discipline, self-mastery, and understanding that any art requires. I started on this path when I was eleven years old, and I have pursued it from my homeland all the way to America. I have followed it through numerous fights and encounters on the street. It is a path that has taken me through six national tournaments and an All-Japan Championship title. I have no expectations that anyone else will live the same way I do, but I will not alter my own conduct to suit someone else's fancy. The desire of this total stranger to fight with me—only because I was a former karate champion—was a deadly serious matter to me.

I selected a *gi* (training uniform) from the pile next to my desk and changed, unaware that I was standing so close to the front window—I was fully concentrated on the challenge ahead of me. The stranger came out in his gi and warmed up. Out of the corner of my eye I watched him throw a few kicks and punches from a very wide stance. I finished tying my belt and stretched. The stranger continued to warm up in his sideways stance, his feet still spread wide, his weight well back. It was an impressive stance to watch—low and powerful, but not very mobile or quick. It was a style that had been popularized in America by the television show *Kung Fu*. It was a showy, impractical style that belonged on television, but not in the dojo or out on the street.

I watched without expression, mentally calculating my strategy. With his weight back and his front foot extended, his front leg would be very vulnerable to a sweep or low kick. Using a sweep, I could hook his lead leg with my ankle and pull the supporting leg out from beneath him, forcing him to lose balance. The other choice was to attack the front leg with a low roundhouse kick. The impact would divert his attention to the lower part of his body and I would follow up with an attack to the face using a high roundhouse kick. When you first attack low, your opponent's hands inevitably drop, leaving his head open to attack. It took but a second to decide just what I would do, and yet that second of understanding would have been impossible without the hours and years of constant training of both mind and body.

I stood up and walked into the middle of the floor. I stood in the ready stance and bowed briefly to my opponent.

"Ready?"

"Okay," he said.

He dropped into his low, wide stance and moved his hands in small circles in front of his face. He looked comical, pawing the air like a dog paddling in a pond. The faint sound of the lights humming, the traffic in the street—it all went away, and I settled into my own fighting stance. It was like entering another world, always familiar and yet strangely quiet—a world of intense concentration and alertness where I felt neither pain nor fear, a world to which street noises, the shouts of one's friends, or the cheering of a crowd came distantly as if through a thick glass. One never knew what would happen in that world where life occurred in the absolute present. One thing was certain, however: whatever occurred would happen in a perfect solitude that was at once the loneliest, most profound, and most glorious of moments life could offer.

I settled onto the balls of my feet and focused entirely on my opponent's eyes. I allowed my field of vision to expand so that peripherally I could see his arms and legs. The large hands pawed the air in precious circles. He moved slowly back and forth. I timed his movement watching his cold blue eyes. He blinked and I *kiai-ed* from the bottom of my belly. The room shook as I attacked instantly.

I leaped forward, pivoting on my left foot as I drove a low roundhouse kick to the middle of his front thigh. He staggered as my shin drove deep into his muscle. The leg had no place to go, and the muscle absorbed the full impact. Immediately I followed with a second roundhouse kick, this time to the outside of the thigh just above the knee. I kiai-ed again as a third kick caught him square on the jaw with a loud crack. He started falling like a big tree, his eyes wide with disbelief. He landed on his back and stayed there, clutching his leg, groaning. It was over.

The challenge that afternoon in Denver was not the greatest I have ever faced, but still I had to meet it as if it were. It was a challenge that might have ended quite differently, but you can never calculate that ahead of time. You simply confront the challenge head on as if it were your final match. You entrust yourself to your training and spirit and technique. You entrust yourself to the years of preparation, and if that preparation has been done with full attention and love and dedication, you find yourself floating in that momentary solitude. You find that time slows down and you see your opponent's attack before he even cocks his hip or raises his knee. You anticipate his every movement. You penetrate his mind. You own the moment.

In karate, these moments stretch through a lifetime. They reach deep down into the body. They reshape the mind and spirit. These moments can occur in the dojo, in the stadium, or on a lonely hillside, working out, pushing yourself a little further than you thought you could go. Over the years these moments change you a little at a time. They make you a little faster, a little stronger. They build the mind and enlarge the spirit in ways that allow you to take on greater and greater challenges.

Karate is not just winning, but learning and understanding. It is a journey with many beginnings. Thinking only of who is strongest and attempting to prove it in tournaments, sparring, or encounters in the street is the wrong attitude. More important than winning is being able to use karate to look into one's life. This is the real meaning of karate. It is a journey of self-discovery that leads out of the dojo and touches on every facet of life. Whether you have trained for ten years or have never set foot on a dojo floor, the lessons of karate are the lessons of life itself: meeting challenge, focusing the mind, shaping the will, staying open to the forces of nature and blending them to the spirit within. Karate is just another path leading to that internal garden we all carry with us, every moment of every day. It is a way of discovering the best part of ourselves—our own unique spirit. That is what karate teaches and that is what this story is about: one man's journey in karate.

Let us begin.

One

I was born on January 27, 1954, in the small village of Hizuchi, in Yawatahama City on the island of Shikoku.

Hizuchi is a farming community set on the valley floor between two mountains whose steep hillsides are thick with orange, tangerine, and grapefruit orchards. Even though my family owned many acres of fruit trees, we were still very poor. There were ten children to feed, six brothers and four sisters. I was the youngest.

By the age of six I was expected to do my share of the work. I would arrive home after school to find a message written on the little blackboard at the back door, telling me where I was needed. I would run up the hill to join my brothers, often working until well after dark. Running up and down those hills became as natural to me as walking. And without my knowing it, the strength it built grew a little more each day.

It was a strength that I would have to learn to control. And though I didn't know it at the time, I would end up spending most of my life learning techniques to help channel that strength—to give it focus, speed, direction, and timing. It would become a quest that would eventually take me into the dojo and into a life in karate.

I was four years old when this family portrait was taken in 1958. My parents are standing in the center, top row. The youngest of ten children, I am standing at bottom right.

My village of Hizuchi, from one of the surrounding hillside orchards. My house was in the middle of the village.

My father was a carpenter who left the business of raising citrus fruit to my mother, my brothers, and me. If you had told my father on the night I was born that his new son would grow up to be an All-Japan National Champion, he probably would have laughed. As an infant I was so tiny that my father was too embarrassed even to take me out in public. But I started sprouting very quickly. I grew fairly tall, and by the time I was six years old I was the biggest student in my first-grade class. And that year I put my size to good use by winning my first sumo wrestling trophy.

Each year in mid-August, a sumo tournament for the boys was held in my valley at the Buddhist temple. All ages competed according to school grade. I can't remember exactly what happened during my fighting debut. I do recall entering the ring dressed in clean white shorts, tossing the ritual salt, bowing. And when the referee dropped the gunbai (a ceremonial fan), I remember how we rushed together, locked in battle just like our heroes in the magazines. I can still hear the shouts and the sound of my opponent grunting as I tried to shove him out of the straw ring. But how exactly I won, I still can't say. I do know that when the action was over, and they raised my hand, everyone cheered, and I'll never forget how that sound warmed me inside.

I not only won that first year, but every year after that as well. Sumo wrestling became a much-needed release for me. It allowed me to let my strength loose in a constructive way. But sometimes I liked to show off that power, and my brother Masanori would tell me that I used my strength too much. I should learn to use my mind as well, he said.

I didn't believe him until the point was driven home by, of all things, a wheelbarrow. I was ten or so. It was harvest time, and we were all working in one of the upper orchards.

I was guiding a loaded wheelbarrow downhill, when suddenly it began rolling too fast. Fruit spilled over the top as the wheelbarrow gathered speed, crashing between the trees. I dug in my heels and pressed down the handles, harder and harder, with all my might, as the steel supports furrowed through the damp soil. Finally one of the handles broke in my palm, and the runaway wheelbarrow swerved against the hillside and gently came to a stop all by itself.

Luckily no one was hurt. As I caught my breath, surveying the load of bruised oranges dotting the ground, Masanori gently explained that if I had turned the wheelbarrow to one side—the way it wanted to go in the first place—it would have stopped by itself. "You use only your power," he laughed. "Next time, use your head!"

An awareness began to stir inside me that day. I didn't realize it at the moment, but I had just had my first lesson in the martial arts. The methods for turning an opponent's strength to one's advantage wouldn't become fully set in my mind until I started learning judo from Mr. Enmyo Ishida. They wouldn't become a part of my instincts until I began to study karate with Kancho Ashihara. Still, my experience with the wheelbarrow was, in its way, a beginning.

There are two sides to the martial arts—technique and spirit. It would take many years for me to understand how both must be used together in harmony in order to perform well under pressure. My experience with the wheelbarrow taught me the importance of using my power and mind together, and I would spend my life perfecting technique. As for that combination of strength and heart called spirit, it came to me as naturally as standing up for a friend in need.

When I was in fifth grade, there was a sixth grader at our school called Bancho because he always acted like a big shot. Bancho wasn't very tall, but he was tight and wiry, and he wore a menacing scowl that said, "Keep your distance or else!" Even the teachers had trouble keeping him in line.

One day out in the schoolyard, my best friend hurried by with tears in his eyes.

"Matsuoka, what happened?" I asked.

"Bancho!" he wept. "He beat me up for no reason at all." I didn't need to hear another word. I ran inside to the sixth grade room, and when Bancho saw me coming, he got to his feet and crossed his arms contemptuously.

"Why did you beat up Matsuoka?" I demanded.

"I don't know what you're talking about," he sneered. He stuck his hand against my chest and tried to push me away. Just then something inside me exploded. I shoved Bancho as hard as I could, and he tumbled backward, crashing into the row of desks behind him. The desks toppled one by one like giant dominoes. The whole row lay in a shambles, and the room was filled with noise and shouting. I jumped on Bancho's stomach and pinned his arms to the floor. The next thing I knew, the teacher was dragging us to our feet. He ordered Bancho back to his desk but kept watching me, his eyes bright, as the hint of a smile crept into the corners of his mouth. "So, Ninomiya," he said stroking his chin, "you are now fighting the big boss of the whole school, eh?"

If Bancho's teacher was angry about the disturbance I caused in his classroom that day, I never heard another word about it. As for Bancho, he kept his distance and never picked on Matsuoka again. In fact, I never saw him attack another student again.

Even in fifth grade I didn't need to be told there was a right way and a wrong way to use my strength. It would

*My best buddies from the neighborhood. We did
everything together. I'm in back, on top of the post.*

always make more sense to use that power to help people,
instead of making them feel helpless and small.

When I was in sixth grade, Mr. Enmyo Ishida came to
teach history and judo at the junior high school in Hizuchi.
Every afternoon just before classes let out, I would hear the
soft slap of his geta (wooden sandals) moving across the
empty playground, and then Mr. Ishida would appear
dressed in his gi and black belt, making his way to the gym.
Mr. Ishida was about 43 years old when he came to Hizuchi,
a short wide man, very much the judo type I had seen in
magazine photos. He even walked like a judo player, chest
out and shoulders swinging back and forth with each step. I
was very impressed with the powerful way he carried

himself, and each day I looked forward to his regal stroll across the schoolyard.

Although I played all the popular team sports in school, I liked best the individual challenge of running. In sixth and seventh grades I competed in middle distance races and trained every day after school with the team. My legs were already strong from years of running up and down the steep orchards, so I did pretty well in competition against other schools. In seventh grade, however, our running coach left the school. For a few months we tried to train after classes without him, but gradually the team members lost interest and our running program fell apart.

That same year Mr. Ishida had become my teacher for history and homeroom. He was a wonderful teacher who captured our imaginations with vivid descriptions of famous battles and their heroes. He was very strict, but if we finished our daily work early and had done well, he would sing to us in a deep beautiful voice—songs about *samurai* and the fighting spirit of old. It wasn't too long before I was captivated by the samurai spirit, and once our running program ran out of gas, I decided to train in judo with Mr. Ishida.

Mr. Ishida proved even more strict as a judo master than he was in the classroom. He criticized us severely, and if he felt a student was being lazy or not paying attention during training, he would wake him up with a slap across the cheek. I never received one of Mr. Ishida's wake-up calls, because I never felt more alert than when I was training. My eyes were like saucers, and my head was full of new techniques. Those new techniques were merely basic sweeps and throws, but I sensed quickly how they were channeling my power in new directions. When done properly, these techniques felt effortless, as if they were happening by themselves. My lesson with the wheelbarrow took on a whole new meaning. I was learning what it meant to turn an opponent's power against himself. I was also learning the value of mental discipline. I understood that the martial arts as seen from the outside posed a very different experience from the reality on the inside. I could see the effects of challenging myself a little more each day; judo was changing my body and building my spirit.

I couldn't get enough of judo. After practice I would come home and train some more on my own. I would run up to the *Shinto* shrine on the hillside behind our house. In a corner of its isolated garden I would work out. I tied an old bicycle inner tube around the trunk of a tall pine tree, and I would pull on the tube with my shoulders and hips, shaking the top branches as I practiced the movements of the throws I had learned, trying to build my strength. I pulled on that inner tube with all my might, thinking to myself: *One day I'll pull down this tree.*

It never happened, of course. I never did pull down that tree with a crash of limbs snapping, at least not the way I had pictured it. But sure enough, years later, after winning the All-Japan, I returned home and visited the Shinto shrine. And in the corner of its garden where I had spent so many hours training, I found that my pine tree was gone. When I asked my mother what had happened to it, she explained it had been blown down in a storm. "The odd thing is," she added, "it was the only tree damaged. And not only that, it was pulled out cleanly by the roots."

At the end of eighth grade I received my black belt, and around the same time, I also received an introduction to the potential power of another martial art—karate. It occurred through an unfortunate incident that showed me firsthand the misuse of that power. It also revealed the depth of Mr. Ishida's commitment to the martial arts and his very strong sense of honor.

During my eighth-grade year, the captain of the judo team was a ninth grader who had picked up some karate moves from a friend of his. When Mr. Ishida wasn't around, he would occasionally try out his karate before class by flashing a series of punches and kicks under our noses. I was intrigued by his speed and power. His technique was rough, but I could still tell how devastating the results would be if he ever made contact.

One afternoon the captain did make contact. One of his roundhouse kicks caught a lower belt square on the jaw with a loud crack. The boy's jaw was broken. I doubt the captain had intended to hurt the boy; he had merely learned a few techniques and wanted to show off his power. Unfortunately he'd used that power in the wrong way. For me it was an incident that not only demonstrated the awesome force of karate, but later on would make me doubly responsible in the use of that force.

For Mr. Ishida, the consequences were very grave. He was convinced the broken jaw of his student had left a black mark next to his name. To Mr. Ishida, it was a sign that he had failed to transmit the spirit and dedication of the samurai in which he believed so deeply. Although he stayed on at the school, Mr. Ishida never taught judo again.

The judo team continued to practice, and in ninth grade I was named captain. In Mr. Ishida's absence, I was determined to be a strong leader and keep the group together. All that year I trained hard but devoted just as much energy to my studies, in preparation for the high school entrance examinations in February. After training I would come home and study late into the night, then go out into the alley for calisthenics in order to keep myself awake so I could study some more. More than once, I dragged myself out into the rain to do frog jumps in a pair of rubber boots, only to wake up the neighbors: "Ninomiya," they shouted, "go to sleep! Stop flapping around out there like a duck!"

I did well on my exams and was accepted at Yawatahama High School, the finest high school in the area. Everyone was very proud, and I think that even the neighbors forgave my late night calisthenics. But one of the happiest surprises of all occurred one afternoon, when Mr. Ishida arrived at my door. He bowed and handed me a carefully wrapped package. Inside was a black belt with my name embroidered on it. "Now that you are continuing with your judo, you will need this," he explained shyly. Needless to say, I was deeply honored.

Even with all of the advantages of attending the finest high school in the area, there were many new things for me to adjust to. For the first time in my life, I felt self-conscious about my hand-me-down clothes. I was embarrassed by the patches on my pants. Finally I decided not to worry about it: if I didn't have the fanciest clothes, at least I would make the best of what I did have—and that was judo.

The judo program at Yawatahama was one of the best on Shikoku. As demanding as Mr. Ishida was, the training sessions at Yawatahama were twenty times harder. The *senpai* (more advanced players) were very tough and worked the better, younger players especially hard. During calisthenics, as we frog-jumped around the perimeter of the training room, a senpai would often grab the back of my belt and make me pull him and maybe several others along behind me. During sit-ups, a senpai would squat on my knees and pinch my thighs to make me go faster and harder.

After calisthenics we trained in *uchikomi*, the practice of setting up a throwing technique without actually completing

*In my senior year, 1972, I (front row, center) was captain
of the Yawatahama High School judo team.*

*Every year, our judo team paraded before the Field Day
celebration. I am at the far right.*

the throw. Uchikomi literally means "fitting in," or maneu-
vering yourself into a position of superior leverage from
which you control your opponent's balance and can suc-
cessfully throw him. Uchikomi is a muscular chess game of

timing and quickness, using a combination of holds and quick footwork to move your opponent off balance. Once the strategic throwing position is achieved in uchikomi, it is not necessary to actually throw the opponent to the floor; by that point the battle has been decided. But uchikomi can be exhausting work, mentally and physically. Afterward, we had an hour of *randori*—free practice—and I was always paired with the heaviest fighter, who weighed 220 pounds. Finally we finished off each training session with a half hour of *tokkun*, extra training for the most advanced players. Tokkun consisted of escaping and reversing ten different players in a row, each using a different hold. I never failed to win these contests. In fact, in three years of daily training and in all of my high school competitions, I was never defeated. But I paid the price: my ears were rubbed raw from squirming out of one hold after another. On top of that, the senpai never failed to cuff me playfully there just to let me know I had done a good job. To this day my ears are scarred from the beating they took in tokkun.

On weekends and vacations I spent extra hours working out in the gym at the police station in Yawatahama. An off-duty officer, who was an eighth-degree black belt, would coach us. Oddly enough, it was my dedication to judo and these extra sessions at the police station that finally carried me into the path of the man who would change my life entirely—a man who would eventually lead me away from judo and into a life of karate.

It happened one morning when a friend and I walked into the empty dojo at the police station. We found a karate player already working out in front of the mirrors against the far wall. The stranger was a black belt in his early twenties, well built and broad in the shoulders. But something about him was different. I couldn't take my eyes off him.

He didn't move like any karate player I had ever seen before. He was faster and looser; his punches and kicks snapped the air almost invisibly, and he glided on his feet as if hardly touching the ground. Traditionally karate called for spreading the legs wide and planting the feet solidly on the floor—a stance capable of generating great power down low, but one that wasn't very quick or mobile. As the stranger snapped kicks straight up, his foot stopping well behind his head, I kept marveling at his flexibility and speed. I wondered what it would be like if I could use some of that quickness in my judo.

The stranger kept moving like that for another ten or fifteen minutes, flashing precise combinations of kicks, blocks, and punches. He pivoted easily on the balls of his feet, assumed a fighting stance, then blocked and countered with more punches and elbow strikes. His breathing was light. His kiai weren't violently loud, but they filled the room with a low rumbling that vibrated up through the soles of my feet.

No doubt the stranger was aware of us watching him, and when he finally stopped, he walked over with a smile and asked if we were interested in karate.

"A little," I said.

"You look like you have a good body for karate. Let me see your stomach."

I backed away a half step, unused to anyone being so direct. But I liked his friendly manner. I pulled open my gi and tightened my stomach muscles.

"Very nice," he said. Then he made a fist with his right hand. "May I?" he asked politely.

I nodded, and he landed several punches just below my solar plexus.

*I was fourteen-years old when I first met Kancho Ashihara.
One year later I started training in karate.*

"Very good. Very good. You should be taking karate. I have just started teaching classes here. Come down and work out with us," he urged. "You've got a good body—very tight."

Afterwards, I couldn't get the stranger's display of speed and power out of my mind, but I still didn't sign up for karate right away. For one thing, I was still very much dedicated to judo. For another, I was still troubled by the incident in Mr. Ishida's class two years earlier.

Around that time, my brother Norinaga had started training with a new karate teacher in Yawatahama. One day he brought home a book called *Karate for Everyone*, a bestseller that I had seen often but had never bothered to read. I started turning its pages and found some photos of the same stranger I had seen working out at the police station. His name was Hideyuki Ashihara. My brother explained that this man was his new karate teacher; he had opened a Kyokushin branch dojo in town, part of a large network of karate schools. Developed by Mas Oyama, who liked to be photographed meditating under waterfalls and fighting bulls with his bare hands, Kyokushin was known for its tough training regimen and for the All-Japan Tournament held each year in Tokyo. "Look," my brother said, "if you're so curious, why don't you come down and train with Ashihara? You might learn something new."

My brother was right about my learning something new. The very next day I went in and started training with Kancho Ashihara. It was the beginning of a long and very strong relationship.

Two

After my years of judo, karate posed some totally new challenges for me. My hands and feet weren't used to the constant impact of punching and kicking. My hands had never experienced the rigors of knuckle handstands on a hardwood floor, and it took a long time for my shins to become conditioned to the bruising impact of blocking low kicks. But worst of all, judo had gotten me used to concentrating my power inward. As a result, my body was very tight and I had a difficult time loosening up in order to direct that power outward for karate. This was especially true for my legs and hips—I thought I would never be able to throw a high roundhouse kick. After having achieved success in judo, it was very humbling to start over from scratch in karate.

But I wasn't about to give up. I stretched constantly. If I was working on a hardwood floor, I would put towels under my feet so my heels would slide and I could stretch my hips further. I discovered that sandy surfaces helped enormously when it came to spreading the legs and limbering the groin and hamstrings.

Karate was grueling work and training was always very rigorous, but Kancho had a way of poking fun at us to keep us loose. "Ninomiya, your legs are much too short!" he would shout with a comical little grimace. He would illustrate his point by holding his hands about six inches apart in front of his face, as if he were showing the length of a tiny fish. "You have to stretch more to make your legs longer." Then he would move his hands apart to shoulder width. When he suddenly relaxed his features and let out his breath with a loud sigh, it was hard not to understand just what he meant.

I had never run into a sense of humor quite like Kancho's, and I was always surprised by my new teacher's way of putting us all at ease. You never knew when he would interrupt class with a joke, and you also never knew when that joke might be played at your expense. Kancho loved to mimic facial expressions. If you didn't have the face of a matinee idol, or were unfortunate enough to have just come from the barbershop so that your features stuck out awkwardly, not even the gods could save you from Kancho. It might not happen right at the beginning of class. You might be lined up ready to receive instruction on an upper block or a side kick, when suddenly Kancho would stop in his tracks. He would walk over to you, as if he had just heard the worst news in the world. He would stand in front of you, wincing painfully as he closely examined your face. "Oh, my goodness, what happened?" he would ask with great concern. "Were you in an auto accident? Did your face hit the windshield?" Then he would smack his palm against his face, and wince again as the others broke into an uproar of laughter. Of course you couldn't help what a crew cut did to your face. You would turn cherry red and squirm miserably, praying for training to resume. Your only consolation was the knowledge that Kancho spared no one. And after another moment of his antics, you didn't care because you were laughing, yourself, just as hard as anyone else.

I have seen Kancho mimic businessmen, waiters, and policemen alike. He has always done it with good humor and so infectiously that not even the victim can help but laugh. I have often wondered what sort of career Kancho would have had as a comedian, had he not pursued a life in karate. In the dojo his sense of humor helped us keep our training in perspective. His joking lightened the burden of that challenge and always put a sense of play back into our routine. He kept us from taking ourselves too seriously or feeling too important. Most of all, his humor reminded us that we were only human.

Each evening after school I rushed over to the karate dojo and worked out on the heavy bag. I was usually the first one there, and Kancho would later say that he could always tell when I had arrived because he could feel the vibrations from the heavy bag through the floor in his living quarters upstairs.

After training I stayed late with the upper belts and worked on my techniques. Kancho would watch us like a hawk, correcting us and explaining the method behind his system. I wasn't the only one who was impressed by the logic of Kancho's system. Students from all over Japan came to the dojo in Yawatahama to train with Kancho. One year a runner-up in the All-Japan tournament came to train with us; the following year he took Kancho's techniques back to the All-Japan and won the championship. I was constantly surprised by the logic and simplicity of Kancho's style. It was intelligent and practical. He always stressed getting the maximum impact from a minimum amount of force. For example, a sweep countering a high-kick was no longer a matter of muscling an opponent to the floor by kicking him as hard as you could; instead, Kancho explained the importance of timing. He showed us that when an opponent's kicking leg reached its highest point, the supporting leg offered the least resistance. He told us to hook the ankle from the side to reduce that supporting resistance even more. The sweeping low-kick wasn't the only technique that was more effective Kancho's way—they all made good tactical sense.

I was devouring everything I could about Kancho's techniques. I practiced them endlessly and my hard work began to pay off. After my first promotion test I was passed over my yellow belt and awarded a green belt. I resolved to train even twice as hard. There were others at the dojo who shared my passion for training and we became close friends, often going out afterwards for dinner and more talk about karate. Two friends in particular have remained close to me over the years—Noriyoshi Nakamoto and Senpai Hiroyasu Kono.

When I started training at the Yawatahama dojo, Shihan Noriyoshi Nakamoto was a brown belt. Today he is *shihan* (teacher and trainer of teachers) in charge of that dojo and supervises several others in the area. A quiet man who possesses a strong spirit, he has trained in karate for more than thirty years, and the example of his hard work and patience has always been an inspiration to me.

Mr. Hiroyasu Kono was a green belt when I started training with Kancho. He was some years older than I, and his generosity provided me with many a late-night meal and countless rides home from town. More than that, his constant friendship and words of encouragement over the years have seen me through some difficult times.

With these two friends I visited the *ramen* (noodle) shops in town and talked karate after training. We supported one another and urged each other on to greater and greater challenges. I was very lucky to have these senpai looking after me during my first years in karate. They considered me more than just another student, and today I still count them among my closest friends.

I will always cherish those early days training at the dojo in Yawatahama. It was the beginning of my life in karate. And thanks to Kancho, it was also the start of my education in life outside the dojo. Even though he wasn't wealthy at the time, Kancho would take out the brown and black belts about once a month for a meal of Korean barbecue. For me it was a luxury. I had never eaten meat before in quantity. It was also an education in good manners. Kancho insisted that we learn how to carry ourselves both inside and outside the dojo. He showed us how to share a meal by serving each other and showing the proper courtesies. To this day courtesy is an important part of my training in karate. In fact, the first precept of the *Dojo Kun* (Code of Ethics) mounted on the wall in my Denver headquarters reads: "We will always be courteous and show respect to others."

Kancho was always taking care of others, and his generosity extended beyond good meals in restaurants. My first pair of leather shoes came from Kancho, as did numerous shirts and pairs of trousers passed on from his wardrobe. The dojo began to feel more and more like my home away from home, and I realized that my friends there—Mr. Kono, Shihan Nakamoto, and Kancho Ashihara—were all part of a growing family.

Between my daily training in judo and another two and a half hours of karate at night, I might have bitten off more than I could chew, but the long hours of training didn't seem to hurt my performance in judo or karate.

*Our village sumo team won the regional championship when
I was sixteen. My brother Masanori (second row left)
and I (second row right) are holding prizes.*

School, however, was another matter. I stayed up late, got
my work done all right, and handed it in on time. My only
problem was staying awake during classes: I couldn't keep
my eyes open. I became an expert at sleeping in a sitting
position. I would sit up very straight, with my book open in
front of me, so that when I closed my eyes it would appear
to the teacher that I was diligently reading the text. The trick
always worked like a charm—until I started snoring. Then
the teacher would wake me up and ask very politely if I
wouldn't mind following along with my eyes open. Try as I
might, I just couldn't stay awake. The teachers all knew that
I was on the judo team and were well aware of the rigors of
our training schedule, though they probably didn't know I

was also training in karate. At any rate, after a while they became either so forgiving or so fed up that they finally just let me sleep in class as long as I didn't snore.

During my junior year I found a motorbike in a junk yard and patched it together so it would run well enough to get me into town and home again at the end of the day. Motorbikes weren't allowed at my high school, so I had to ride it into town and park a block away from the school. I was very proud of my motorbike. I painted it silver gray, the same color as the police motor scooters. I even attached a mudguard to the back fender that had the name of our karate school on it. I thought I looked very cool. The only problem with my beloved motorbike was that it refused to start. The kick-starter never did work, and in order to get the thing going, I had to run it down the street, jump aboard, pop the clutch, and hit the gas. With some luck and a little prayer, the engine would catch and I would be on my way. But if it didn't work, I would have to get off and give it another running start.

I was sixteen and "street legal." Kancho Ashihara teased that I spent more time running alongside my motorcycle than riding it.

I think Kancho was always very amused by my little scooter. He would always ask me if I had "run my scooter" into town. He teased me sometimes: "Ninomiya, what's the sense of having a motor scooter if you have to run alongside it instead of riding on the seat like most people?" Kancho knew the answer, of course. He knew I was proud of that motor scooter and that I was determined to make it run any way I could.

All along, I think Kancho sensed that I wasn't like most people. My determination and my dreams were different. I think Kancho and I were both different from most of the people around us, and that difference drew us together in an unspoken way. For one thing, I think Kancho and I both knew what we wanted out of life, and we were both willing to go to great efforts to have it. As a teacher he taught me to reach those goals. He encouraged me to believe in my dreams and showed me how to make them come true. Let me explain.

Like most people who come from a small village, I had often wondered what it would be like to live in a big city. The big cities I dreamed about, however, were always in America. Maybe it was the pictures of the open spaces around those cities that captivated me—the forests, plains, and snow-capped mountains. But more than that sense of space was the freedom to live the way I wanted.

In Japan there was never enough space or freedom. Land was so precious and the homes so small that we Japanese jokingly called them "rabbit hutches." My family of twelve shared a three-bedroom house. Even in our farming village, homes were built side by side and privacy was at a premium. Loudspeakers posted throughout the village awakened us in the morning. Throughout the day the announcer told us what meetings to attend and what activities had been planned. We wore uniforms to school, we vacationed in groups, and even married by arrangement. If you were well educated and landed a job with a big corporation, you were expected to stay with that company for a lifetime. For a Japanese, the burdens of tradition and conformity were enormous. I can't say why, but from a very young age I dreamed of a different kind of life—one with greater freedom and more choice. The movies I saw and the books I read all kept connecting that dream of freedom to America. To my seventeen-year-old mind, America wasn't even a country so much as a state of mind where anything seemed possible. For years I had dreamed of this special place across the ocean. I never talked about it much with my friends, but privately I always fantasized about going there.

Shortly after I was passed to green belt, I became increasingly aware that Kancho was keeping an eye on me. At the time I was physically his biggest student. He would give me additional help after class and in some ways made more demands of me than he did of the others. I'm not sure how the subject of my going to America came up, but one evening after training Kancho took me aside and told me that he too had dreamed of going there. He said that it had almost happened once, but things hadn't worked out. Then he said, "If you want to go to the U.S., I can help you make that happen." He was encouraging me to follow what had been his dream as well. In some ways I felt that Kancho was handing something to me that evening—the possibility of reaching my goal. It wasn't just a fantasy anymore. He hadn't said it in so many words, but I knew that karate would be the tool to help me make that dream come true.

When I was seventeen, I earned my brown belt in karate. I was in eleventh grade, and that same year Kancho chose me along with five others from our dojo to fight in the All-Japan Open Karate Tournament. I was the youngest in the whole tournament.

My brothers were proud of my selection, but my parents worried about my missing semester exams. They thought karate was taking away too much of my time from my studies. As it was, I often came home from training after they had gone to sleep; my mother would leave a plate of food for me on the stove. Despite their concern, my parents knew how dedicated I was and never discouraged me. They wouldn't be able to come to Tokyo with me, but they wished me well. When I heard that the others in our dojo were all planning to fly to Tokyo for the tournament, I knew my family wouldn't have the money to pay for a plane ticket. I confessed this to Kancho, who told me not to worry because he would take care of it for me.

A jumping side kick at a Yawatahama karate demonstration, my senior year of high school.

Kancho's generosity took a great weight off my mind, but there were other, little things that made me edgy about that first trip. I had never been on a plane before and spent the whole flight glued to the window. I had been to Tokyo once before on a school excursion, but I was still worried about getting swallowed up in the crowds and separated from the group. Finally the morning of the tournament arrived and I only had to think about karate.

We had trained hard in preparation for the tournament, and when the time came I felt as ready as I possibly could. I had been competing in judo for several years by that point, so I wasn't nervous at the prospect of fighting in front of a large crowd. But I was seventeen years old, with not quite two years of training in karate under my belt, and I was about to face the best competition in the world. Although Kancho no longer competed, he had expressed to me his attitude about competition many times before. It was the same advice he gave in the face of any challenge. Once again he took me aside. He looked me in the eye and quietly said, "Only the gods can give 100 percent. But if you try to give 120 percent, you might come close to giving your all." I intended to do just that.

In my first round match I faced a fighter who was my same size. I was able to display a variety of techniques and finally won by knocking him down with a low sweep. The second round wouldn't be so easy. I faced Mr. Katusaki Sato. He was taller and heavier than I, and I knew from the program that he had also attained a fourth degree black belt in judo. His build was very much the judo type—powerful legs and low center of gravity—combined with the flexibility and speed of karate. Again I tried a number of different techniques—particularly low kicks—but nothing seemed to work because my opponent was so big. In return, Mr. Sato came at me repeatedly with the combination of a left *mawashi geri* (roundhouse kick) and a right *ushiro geri* (straight back kick), followed by a series of punches. He failed to put me down, however, and our match was sent into overtime. In the overtime period we both continued with the same tactics, but neither one of us emerged the clear winner; the referees called for a second overtime. At this point I was running out of strength. The sound of the crowd, the encouragement of my coach—everything began to sound very far off. The round began and I felt very slow. My hands were dropping. For the first time ever I was beginning to think I had had enough. Even before the judges had decided the match and awarded Mr. Sato the victory on points, I sensed that I had lost the mental contest. Privately, I had admitted my fatigue. Although I fought on to the finish, in my own mind I had given in to exhaustion and had already conceded the match. That evening Mr. Sato went on to win the All-Japan.

The next morning our group from Yawatahama flew home. As I sat quietly looking out the window of the plane, I thought over the events of the last twenty-four hours. I had been defeated in my first All-Japan tournament; but I knew, with all due respect to Mr. Sato's technique and strength, that I had in part defeated myself. However, I decided not to dwell on that defeat. I resolved to think of my match with Mr. Sato as a major building experience. Shortly after that match, Kancho had offered a few simple words of encouragement and told me that I needed more training to build my stamina. That evening after our flight home, my body was aching and my shins were still sore, but I was back in the dojo. I was already preparing for next year's tournament.

My friends Mr. Kono and Shihan Nakamoto had also been eliminated in the tournament. To commiserate, the three of us went out for dinner after training that first evening back. It was a solemn occasion, yet an important one, because we encouraged one another to challenge ourselves even harder. We vowed to do better the next year. We promised to give 120 percent. That evening I swore to myself that one day I would win the All-Japan.

I have always been very particular about my form, and I learned early on that with Kancho's brand of karate there was always a good reason for doing things the right way. If something in your technique didn't add up, however, Kancho would spot it immediately with his eagle eye, and he had a way of explaining it so you understood and wouldn't forget a second time.

When I was still a brown belt, I had gotten into the bad habit of dropping my hands during *kumite* (fighting). One afternoon I was having a hard time concentrating, and Kancho had to stop me several times to remind me: "Keep your hands up, Ninomiya. Hands up!" But I kept forgetting, and each time my kumite partner took advantage by slapping me lightly on the cheek. With each slap I winced because I had two decayed molars on either side of my mouth. The cavities were very painful, but I had to put off going to the dentist because I simply couldn't afford to pay for professional dental work.

After I dropped my hands for the fourth time, Kancho told my partner to step aside and took his place, assuming the fighting position as I waited for his attack. In a blur Kancho stepped to my right side and punched me in the jaw with a lightning jab that I never even saw. I felt it, though: the pain in my molar shot down to the soles of my feet. We squared off again, and this time I was prepared for Kancho to step to my right. I kept my right hand up high, but in the blink of an eye Kancho went to my left instead. This time the pain in my other sore tooth shot through my body like an electric shock. We sparred for another few minutes until I started keeping both hands up to protect my face. Satisfied that I had learned my lesson, Kancho said we were finished and bowed.

My teeth were no longer sore, but the inside of my mouth was full of something gritty as if I had been fed a spoonful of sand. I spat out the foreign matter into my hand and found little pieces of tooth: Kancho had cleanly knocked out both decayed molars! When I held up my hand and showed him, he told me to open wide and examined the inside of my mouth. "You should be grateful," he said. "No shots, no gas, and I didn't even make you sit in the waiting room." Everyone laughed, but then Kancho pointed his finger at me and frowned: "I warn you, Ninomiya. Keep your hands up, because next time you might face a dentist who will try to take out some of your good teeth instead." I learned my lesson: from that day on, no matter how tired or worn down I've been in a match, I have kept my hands up.

The longer you train in karate, the more you learn about yourself. You also learn a greater respect and appreciation for your teacher—providing that teacher is good. One way of measuring your teacher's worth is to gauge the level of respect he is accorded by other karate players. In Kancho's case, that respect was enormous. There were many karate players who had either studied with Kancho in the past or knew him by reputation for his ability to develop and teach new, practical fighting techniques. Often they would show up at the dojo in Yawatahama to work on their form or to learn some of Kancho's new techniques.

At seventeen, shortly before being humbled by Australian John Jarvis in our sparring bout at the Yawatahama dojo.

John Jarvis was a karate instructor from New Zealand who had studied with Kancho in Tokyo. When I was a brown belt, he came to Yawatahama for two weeks to work again with Kancho. Jarvis was more than six feet tall and strongly built, with long, powerful legs. He insisted that the only man who could teach him anything about karate was Kancho.

One day during training, Kancho paired me with Jarvis during kumite. I felt very awkward. I had never talked to a foreigner before—very few of them had ever come to Yawatahama. Now I was about to spar with one. I'm sure Kancho had chosen me to face Jarvis because I was the biggest student in the dojo. But suddenly I felt like a midget: Jarvis's hips seemed to loom somewhere above my chest, and when I tried to stare him in the eye, I felt as if I were looking into his belly button.

We bowed, and Kancho gave the command to begin fighting. Immediately I attacked with several low kicks followed by a left front kick. But as soon as I straightened my leg,

Jarvis grabbed my ankle, lifted my leg, and shoved me backward. I tumbled into the corner and lay sprawled there like a rag doll. Inside, I was furious, but I wasn't about to let this stranger make a fool of me in my own dojo. I jumped to my feet and came after him again, but I still wasn't able to penetrate his defenses. He deflected everything I threw at him. Finally Kancho told us to stop. I had fought terribly. Jarvis had made me look like a midget white belt. I knew Kancho had expected more from me. He knew how much I still wanted to take Jarvis apart, but he had already let me have my chance. Now he was going to let me sit on my fury and show me how it should have been done. He tried to cool me down first with a joke: "Ninomiya, did you forget to wake up this morning?"

I didn't see the humor. I was furious. I stared down at the floor, my fist still clenched.

"Let me show you how," Kancho said. I moved aside.

Everyone gathered in a circle around Kancho and Jarvis as they faced each other in the middle of the room. They bowed to one another, assumed the fighting stance, and the room went very still. Two seconds later, it was over: Jarvis was on the floor, bleeding from the nose and mouth, the front of his gi covered with blood.

It had happened so fast that I had to go over carefully in my mind what I had just seen: Jarvis had thrown a right-hand punch. Kancho had blocked it, stepped outside with catlike quickness, then driven an uppercut to Jarvis' chin. Jarvis was stunned, and before he could react Kancho had lifted him and thrown him over his shoulder in a *ganseki-otoshi*, a hold similar to a fireman's carry. Jarvis landed on his head.

As the rest of us stood there gaping, Jarvis got to his feet. I knew that, inside, Jarvis was eating crow, choking on his own humiliation and probably cursing Kancho as I had cursed Jarvis only a minute before. On the outside, though, Jarvis was all courtesy and respect. He bowed, thanking Kancho for the lesson, and Kancho told him to wash his face.

Kancho's demonstration didn't make me feel any better. He had cut the New Zealander down to size in a way that I would have given my right arm to have done myself. Now it all just made me angry to see how much further I had to go. I wondered if I would ever have that kind of skill—even half the speed and power I had seen in Kancho. It seemed hopeless.

Although I had seen Kancho sparring in the dojo, I had never seen him face off against a fighter of greater ability than his students. The speed and strength by which he had brought down the tall New Zealander made me respect him in a new way, but it also made me resent him, too.

I don't think I let it show, but inside I was a storm of confusion and anger. For the first time I seriously doubted my own abilities. I questioned this journey I had undertaken. Would I ever reach my goal? Would I ever be able to put away a Jarvis? What was the use of even trying? I had just about hit the bottom. It was one of the lowest points I would ever face in karate. I was out of patience and desire. I didn't know if I would ever bounce back, and I almost didn't care.

The run-in with Jarvis had embarrassed me. I felt as though I had burned out on karate. I wanted to get away. I needed time to think things through. In the dojo I was going through the motions of training, but at the same time I was still feeling a great deal of anger.

I had worked hard on technique over the years, but now it was time to develop my spirit. Spirit was something that had once come quite naturally when it was a matter of standing up to the school bully. But somehow, in the dojo, concentrating so hard on technique, I had let that spirit lapse. Now it was time to build this other half of my art. It was time to develop a mental attitude that would carry me through the most difficult challenge. I didn't have it in my first All-Japan. It wasn't there when I faced Jarvis. Now I would have to find it.

I had reached a point where I felt that I could learn only so much in the dojo. I needed to be on my own, away from family and friends. I needed to build that spirit from the inside out. Not even the greatest teacher in the world could do that for me.

When school let out that August, I decided to go away by myself. I told my parents where I was going, but without a word to anyone at the dojo, I packed up some camping gear, a punching bag, and a few books, and I went to a beach and lived alone for three weeks.

Part of Japan's longest peninsula, separating the Pacific Ocean from the Sea of Japan, Kawanohama Beach was about an hour from my home by motorbike. It was a long, beautiful stretch of fine white sand, with an area in the middle that was popular with swimmers. I pitched my camp at one end of the beach, away from the swimmers, in a group of trees that would provide shade in the hot afternoons. There were no homes around, no distractions, only a vegetable garden and a farmer's field at the base of the mountain across the road.

In the morning I would run, then do push-ups and frog jumps in the sand. Standing knee-deep in the surf, I would practice my kicks. My workouts on the beach were three times harder than they were on the smooth dojo floor, and in just a few days my legs felt even stronger.

At noon, I'd build a fire and cook a meal of rice or noodles. Afterwards, I relaxed in the shade and read. In the late afternoon, I would train some more. I tied my heavy bag to one of the pine trees and I would work out, hammering the bag steadily with combinations of kicks and punches.

For three weeks I talked to no one. Without a word, I watched the swimmers from a distance. I saw the farm woman who came to tend the garden nearby. I felt like Musashi Miyamoto must have felt, alone in his precious mountains, challenging himself to climb the highest peak. Always a model for me, Musashi was the greatest of the chivalrous samurai who wandered the countryside in the late sixteenth and early seventeenth centuries. Living by a strict warrior's code called *bushido*, he perfected his art through meditation, practice, and countless duels. His only companions were his sword and nature. Under the blue sky of Kawanohama Beach, with the endless whisper of the surf in my ears, I was communicating with a deeper spirit, aware only of my breath mingling with the bright air and my energy flowing as one with the elements around me.

Sometimes in the evening, when the sun set and deep shadows fell across the beach, the haunting colors of the orange sky made me feel lonely and a little sad. But a curious thing happened during my stay that raised my spirits and made me feel less alone. In some ways it was as important to me as the training and the solitude, because it told me that what I was doing was right. It made me feel very good inside about my commitment to karate, and it helped make those three weeks at Kawanohama Beach a very special part of my life. It happened after the first few days: I came back from my morning workout on the beach, and at the entrance to my tent I found a small basket filled with fresh eggs. Nobody was nearby, no note had been left behind with the basket. I had no idea who could have been so kind. It made me feel warm inside to think that somebody was looking after me. The eggs were a welcome addition to my diet. I fried them. I boiled some of them. I was working my body hard, and the protein certainly helped rebuild my strength. By the end of the day I had devoured the whole basketful.

The next morning when I returned from the beach, I again found a basket of eggs sitting at the opening to my tent. This went on almost every day during my stay on Kawanohama Beach, and I wondered if I would ever discover the identity of my mysterious benefactor.

One of my last mornings at the beach, I returned to my tent and found the eggs as usual, but this time they had been left for me in a manila envelope. I tore off the name and address written in the corner and decided that if I would never stand face-to-face with my benefactor, at least I could send a note of thanks.

I wrote the letter as soon as I returned home, and a few days later I received a note back. It was from the farm woman who had come to work in the garden near my tent. She wrote that usually she had seen young people come to the beach only to play. She said it made her feel good to see a young person training and studying so hard, and that was why she had left the eggs for me.

I had gone to Kawanohama Beach in part to decide my commitment to karate. The gift of eggs from the thoughtful farm woman came as a form of encouragement that helped me to rededicate myself to the spirit of my art. I decided that one day I would thank this woman in person. Little did I know it would take me twenty-five years.

I returned home stronger in body and mind, and when I walked into the dojo my first day back, Kancho took one look at me and smiled. I had gone away without telling him that I was leaving or where I was going. Now my skin was deep brown and my eyes were bright. "Ninomiya, did you have a good time playing on the beach?" Kancho asked. But I knew that he could see that something inside me had changed. In response to his question, I bowed and took my place in line, prepared to train harder than ever.

On October 22, 1972, I fought in my second All-Japan tournament. In spite of giving everything I had, I lost in the third round to a *san-dan* (third degree black belt) who was a fourteen-year veteran in karate and later lost to the tournament champion, Miyuki Miura. Again I felt the same frustration at my own letdown of spirit. Once again I hadn't pushed myself hard enough. I wondered if I would ever be able to climb beyond fatigue. I knew there was a clarity of spirit that lifted fighters out of themselves to a level of performance surpassing normal limitations. I had glimpsed that spirit, but holding to it in the face of the toughest challenge was another matter. *Mushin*—no mind, the ability to perform beyond technique or conditioning without regard to self or other—I wondered if I would ever find that quality in myself. At those times of my deepest frustration, it seemed like a fantasy. Mushin was just a clever myth dreamed up to entertain gullible boys who liked to hear stories about warriors and their magical powers.

Despite the waves of disillusionment that would sometimes wash over me, despite the anger and impatience I sometimes felt, I continued to train hard. Not two days after the tournament I was already thinking about next year's All-Japan.

At age seventeen, kickboxing in Yawatahama.

Toward the end of my senior year, recruiters from two or three colleges came around and talked to me about the judo programs at their schools. There was no question in my mind: I had already decided on karate. Karate would be my life. I still wanted more than anything to go to America and I wanted karate to take me there. Judo would end for me with graduation from high school. Maybe it was the disappointment of my performance in the All-Japan. Maybe it was the humiliation I faced at the hands of Jarvis. All I knew was that karate posed more of a challenge for me than judo, as if each setback made me try that much harder. There was also Kancho—I would never find another teacher like him. In my mind, there was no question but that I would continue to train in karate.

After graduation Kancho helped me find a job at the Shikoku headquarters for Goyo Construction in Matsuyama, about an hour from Yawatahama. Goyo very generously accepted me without the usual series of examinations. It was a terrific opportunity for me to be working with one of the top corporations in the world and still train in karate. I moved to Matsuyama and was assigned a room in one of the Goyo dormitories. Goyo provided food, housing, gas— everything I needed or wanted . . . or so I thought.

The problem was that I soon discovered I just wasn't cut out for corporate life. Every day I kept accounts and calculated figures on my abacus. I would sit at the same desk in a roomful of workers performing the same kind of task. My shoulders ached. My necktie choked me. I couldn't keep my mind on the figures in front of me. I kept thinking about karate, and I would count the minutes until quitting time so I could get into the dojo and start moving my muscles again.

After three months at Goyo, the company wanted to transfer me to a job site on the opposite side of the island. I respectfully told them that I wanted to stay in Matsuyama. I couldn't think of moving away from the dojo and training on my own without the benefit of Kancho's teaching. A few months went by and they asked again if I was ready to be sent to one of the site offices. Clearly I would have to make a decision. Goyo had been very generous to me. I admired the company, yet I still felt the need to fulfill my life in karate. My decision was final. I submitted a letter of resignation and brought it to the assistant manager. He sat me down in his office and we talked over my situation. I told him my dream of going to the United States and having my own dojo.

"Are you sure that's not just a kid's dream?" the assistant manager asked.

"I don't think so," I answered. "I have given it a lot of thought. It is what I want more than anything else."

"It's very difficult to succeed in karate," he said. "You know it's very competitive and very hard work."

"I'm sorry, my mind's made up," I said. "It's a difficult decision for me to leave, but I must finish what I have set out to do."

He nodded. "It's your life. Maybe someday you will win the All-Japan. I wish you luck. Everyone here at Goyo will be cheering for you."

No matter what the assistant manager thought of my chances of getting to America, I promised to make that "kid's dream" come true.

When I left Goyo, Kancho rented a little apartment for me not far from the dojo. It was just an empty room with a window and a door—no running water, no stove, nothing. I had been spoiled in the Goyo dormitory. My new place had a community bathroom downstairs next to the manager's office. When the manager locked up at night, the bathroom closed, too. If I had to empty my bladder, I had to jog up to the roof and pee in the gutter. If my bowels started to rumble, I had to run over to the park and use one of the public restrooms. I lived on a diet of rice and noodles. Meat was out of the question.

I trained day and night. In the morning I ran up to Matsuyama Castle. I ran wind sprints in the sandy garden surrounding its walls. In the afternoons I worked out at a weight center. I was hired part-time as an instructor there and also taught karate at one of the university clubs. I hung a bag up on the roof and worked out on it constantly. I used the rail on the roof ledge to practice my kicks—two hundred of each, every day.

At first I didn't regret my decision to leave Goyo. I felt much better, in fact. I was nineteen years old. Kancho had given me my black belt at the end of my high school year. In another four years, if I trained hard, I would be sent to America or Europe. That was the pattern. That was what I was counting on. I wished I could speed things up, but I didn't shortcut my training. I stayed late after every class and worked over my techniques again and again. By now, in addition to his school in Yawatahama, Kancho was teaching at a dojo in Matsuyama. I continued to train under him three times a week. There was nothing else in my life, only karate and the physical challenge of pushing myself to the limit. Sometimes those limits weighed on me physically and mentally. I could take the physical punishment—the hours of training and sweating. But I hated running to the park just to go to the public toilet. I hated jogging to the roof for a pot of water. I hated my diet of ramen and rice. When things became unbearable I asked myself, "Why am I doing this?

Why make life so hard? If I had a job and saved my money, I could go to America on my own. Why do it the hard way?"

When I had reached rock bottom, I came across a cartoon story in a karate magazine about an episode in Mas Oyama's training when he was a young man. He, too, had become discouraged by the hardships of training in the dojo and decided to go to the mountains to rededicate himself to his practice. But after a while he had become even more dejected by the new discipline that he had imposed on himself. Just when he had reached his lowest point, a letter came from his mentor. "I understand the hardship you have imposed on yourself," his mentor wrote. "But remember: although most people think an artist has genius, which allows him to reach perfection, it is, in fact, his perseverance and patience that allow him to succeed. I believe you will be one of the leaders in martial arts in Japan in the future. If you do more than others in your training, no one will be able to compete with your achievements. You will be the best martial artist of your generation."

After receiving this letter, Mas Oyama was inspired to continue training. In order to demonstrate his commitment and to avoid any further lapses of will, he shaved off one eyebrow. He knew that by having only one eyebrow he would not come down from the mountain to where other people might see him, for fear of looking like a freak. He would have to stay and train until the eyebrow grew back.

When I read the cartoon story, I was inspired by Mas Oyama's example. I understood that talent alone was not sufficient; only hard work and effort could make my dreams come true—they were like the water that makes a flower grow. I went up to the roof and wrote with a marking pen in big bold letters on the top of my heavy bag: "Genius alone is

never enough. Only effort makes the artist succeed."
Although no one else would ever see it, I too had "shaved
my eyebrow" that day. It has stayed off ever since.

Whenever things seemed most unbearable, Kancho
would arrive at my door, as if he knew instinctively that I
needed encouragement. He would walk into my apartment
and look at my cupboards filled with rice. He didn't talk
about what I was going through. He didn't need to. He would
simply say, "You need to put on weight, Ninomiya. Let's eat."

The next thing I knew, we were out the door on our way
to a restaurant where he stuffed me full of meat and fish. He
never left without giving me a little cash to buy something
for my cupboards besides rice. Without Kancho I never
would have made it through this period. It was one of the
hardest times of my life, and today my eyes still warm at his
generosity and encouragement during those tough days in
Matsuyama. It cemented my loyalty to Kancho and made me
care for him like a father. In the samurai tradition there is a
saying that if you really and truly care for somebody, you
would be willing to give up your life for that person. I felt
that strongly for my teacher.

On one of his visits, Kancho told me that a nightclub
owner in Matsuyama had expressed interest in hiring one of
his karate students as a security guard. He offered me the
job and explained that if I did well, it might provide a chance
for some of the other students to make some extra money at
a few of the other clubs in town.

I went to work at a place called the Sachimo House, a two-
story disco in the nightclub district. I worked each night
from eight until two in the morning. They had me dress up

in a long navy blue coat with braided epaulets and a fancy hat. I carried a whistle, and I was supposed to stand at attention inside the front door to be available in case any of the customers had too much to drink and made trouble.

The host would stand in front of me and greet the customers as they walked in the door. The customers always stared at me as if I were a doll. Without fail, the girls would walk in with their boyfriends, take one look at me, and ask, "Is he real?" Sometimes they even reached up and tried to touch my face, just to make sure. After a few nights of this, I started blinking just as they reached out to touch me. I can't describe the fun I had watching the terror in their faces as they nearly jumped out of their panty hose and ran squealing into their boyfriends' arms.

There really wasn't much else to keep me busy at the Sachimo House, and when I complained to Kancho that I had nothing to do but stand still and stare straight ahead like a mannequin, he told me to practice my standing meditation.

One night we had a packed house, and I was called upstairs to break up a fight. I jumped at the chance to do something useful for a change and hurried up to the bar, where I collared a punk in black shiny pants with a black *gakusei-huku* (student uniform) jacket. I brought him downstairs, showed him to the door, and pushed him outside. "I'm sorry," I said. "You can't come back in here." He told me to get screwed, offered a few other suggestions, and then ran off down the sidewalk.

I didn't think much about it until a few minutes later when the same character reappeared at the door. He was holding his coat closed this time, and as he tried to push his way through the knot of people waiting outside, I spotted a sword handle sticking out of his collar. It was time for the fancy mannequin to earn his keep.

At nineteen I left Goyo Construction and was training with Kancho Ashiahara in Matsuyama. In the evenings I worked as a security guard at the Sachimo House nightclub.

I squeezed by the host and shoved the punk back outside onto the sidewalk. I followed him out. "You're not going to stop me this time," he threatened. And then he pulled the sword out of his jacket. The blade gleamed, and I felt a cold thin feeling that strung my nerves tight as piano wire. Somehow the sword seemed to be talking to me, as if to say, "Here I am. This is what sharpened steel feels like when it sinks into flesh. Stop me if you can."

I didn't have time to be scared. Before I knew it, the punk had raised the sword and was lunging at me. I stepped to the side, grabbed his hands, and drove a knee kick into his solar plexus. He doubled over and I hooked his leg, pushed his chin back, and kneed him in the back of the head. As he crumpled, the sword clattered to the pavement, and I seized it.

A minute later, as he got to his feet, rubbing the back of his head, I noticed on the inside of his coat the insignia for one of the college karate clubs. "You're very strong!" he said, shaking his head. "I never ran into anyone like you!"

"Make sure it doesn't happen again," I warned. "Next time you might end up eating that fancy sword." Once the situation was under control, my boss came running out of the club and slapped me on the back. He told me I had done a first-rate job. A few weeks later, several other students from the dojo were hired for other clubs around the city.

As for the punk, he never showed his face at the Sachimo again, at least not while I worked there. It was just as well; I had never faced a blade before and wasn't too keen on making it a habit. Still, the challenge at the Sachimo House whetted my appetite for a different kind of contest. And before long I was going out to look for those challenges on my own.

Soon after my run-in with the "college samurai," I overheard some of the students at training talking about the various dojos in town, ranking them according to how tough they were. This piqued my interest. I had always stayed out of such discussions, but this time I made mental notes about which dojos seemed most respected. I decided to visit them and challenge their best fighters.

I suppose everyone who trains in karate is curious about how well his or her style matches up against another. In my case it wasn't curiosity about my style, but more a desire to face the raw challenge of walking into a strange setting and making myself fight as though my life depended on it.

I had watched fighters who came to challenge Kancho at the dojo in Yawatahama, and Kancho had always taken these challenges very seriously. He believed that if a school was to have a true karate spirit, then it must accept a challenge from anyone. On such occasions, Kancho would stop class, sit everyone down, and either have one of his black belts face the challenger or square off himself. There were no rules for such encounters, but the results were inevitably the same; the challenger ended up laid out senseless on the wooden floor, barely breathing, after having been crushed by one of Kancho's techniques.

There was always in such challenges the distinct possibility that you could be seriously injured. But facing up to that possibility and accepting it totally is perhaps the most difficult challenge in karate. It may also be the most necessary. Technique can be learned with the mind, but it will take you only so far in kumite. It may sound extreme to say so, but the fighting spirit that takes you beyond technique comes only from a complete acceptance of the consequences of one's actions—even one's death. I believed then that fighting spirit could be forged in no other way. In my own mind, I had arrived at a point in my karate where my spirit would advance no further unless I confronted my deepest fear. It was time to put myself on the line.

I'm not saying others should go to dojos and make the same challenges I did. At the time, it was the only way I knew to push myself to another plateau. But I don't recommend it now to my own students. I believe that it is better to keep one's strength inside instead of showing it off, just as it is better to keep a sharpened sword in its scabbard than to flourish it unnecessarily. But in those days I was younger, headstrong, and a little arrogant. It seemed very important to prove myself.

I wish I could say I faced those dojo challenges with all of the even-tempered calm of a veteran samurai. From the outside I may have appeared very composed, but a storm of emotions raged inside me. Each time I arrived in front of a strange dojo, I would try to spend a few minutes loosening up before going inside. I would stretch and shake my limbs. I would punch and kick until I had broken a cold sweat, but still my heart would pound and the nagging ache of fear would chill me to the bone.

Imagine my surprise, then, when I walked into my first challenge only to be flatly told by the teacher: "My school doesn't fight with other schools. We won't take your challenge!" I was astonished. Had I been Kancho, I might have insulted their courage. I might have teased them into fighting with me. But words didn't come as quickly to me as they did to my teacher in such situations. I bowed and left, going home to wait until the next night and the next dojo.

It took several frustrating nights, but finally I found a dojo that would accept my challenge. It was housed in a two-story office building on the other side of town. When I arrived it was almost dark. I warmed up in front, as usual, stretching under the trees. I wore a white belt and a plain white gi with all of the dojo insignias stripped off—after all, if I lost, I didn't want it to reflect poorly on Kancho. As I loosened up, I fought the same old fight with myself, trying to conquer my fear. And once I had figured out that getting beaten up by my own fear was probably rougher than the actual kumite I would face inside, I knew I was ready.

I walked firmly inside the dojo and found twenty-five students who had just finished training. The black belts were working out on their own, and the teacher was still sitting at the front of the room, his arms crossed imperiously. I walked right up to him, bowed courteously, and announced that I would like to challenge his best fighter. He puffed up very proudly and smiled mockingly. Then he asked how long and where I had been training. I made up a story about training on my own in back of my house. I told him I was looking for matches but couldn't find any fighters for kumite. When I finished, he laughed, then pounded his heel on the floor. The room went silent and everyone looked up. "Funny guy here wants to fight," said the teacher. "Who wants to take him on?" All of his black belts stepped forward, eager to have at me. He called out the biggest one, and told us to square off.

All the students gathered around, but after I knocked out the first fighter, the teacher jumped to his feet, shouting at the lower belts: "What are you still doing here? Go home!" They all ran off toward the locker room, but I could see their faces peeking out between the slats in the wooden screen.

I threw the second fighter against the wall. His knees buckled, and he slithered to the floor like a sheet of paper. By the time I had finished with the third one, all of the black belts had disappeared. The room was empty except for the teacher and me. I asked him if he would fight me himself.

"I'm very busy," he said gruffly. "I have to go right now! I don't have time!"

He was backing away from my challenge like a cornered animal, and as I stood there feeling a little sad, the image of this pathetic teacher burned into my memory. He was responsible to his students for providing a good example. He was responsible for teaching them more than technique. He should have taught them about spirit as well. Then and there I promised myself that I would never end up like him. I would never be the kind of teacher to back down from a challenge.

There was no need to say another word. I wasn't going to make him fight me if his heart wasn't in it. I bowed and started for the door, and suddenly he called after me: "If you want to fight so much, you should go over to the Ashihara dojo next to the railroad station. They're very strong over there. They'll fight with you!"

I couldn't help smiling. He was talking, of course, about my dojo, but I couldn't very well challenge my own teacher.

A few days later, Kancho called me over after training. "Ninomiya, did you by any chance go challenge another dojo a few days ago?"

I didn't say anything.

"I'll tell you why I ask. Last night I went across town and challenged a teacher at one of the dojos there. Do you know what he told me?"

I shook my head.

"I'll tell you what he said. He told me I was too late. He said that a few days ago a fellow who looked like 'Giant Baba' (an enormous and very popular professional wrestler) had been to his place and torn his students apart. He told me he couldn't afford any more challenges. He didn't even know how he was going to keep the students he had. Ninomiya, was that you?"

"Yes," I said.

Kancho threw up his hands in exasperation. "Ninomiya, next time would you be so kind as to let me know, so I don't waste my time tracing your footsteps! What good is it me for to challenge someone, if you've already beat the stuffing out of them?" He laughed, then walked off still shaking his head.

A week later I passed by the dojo where the teacher had called me "funny guy" and refused my challenge. The windows were dark and a FOR RENT sign hung on the door. I felt a twinge of regret about putting the teacher out of business.

But karate, I thought, should be more than taking money for showing a few techniques. Real karate had no price tag.

If I hadn't been so impatient to get to America, I probably never would have left Goyo. I never would have endured the long hours of training and the hand-to-mouth existence in my waterless flat. I never would have challenged dojo after dojo, testing my spirit. But the fact was I couldn't wait to get to America, and I would have taken on any additional burden as long as it helped me to realize that dream a little faster.

I can't tell you why, but that dream had become the fuel that kept my fires burning inside. Nothing else mattered—not family, not women, not money. Karate was the only thing, and it was going to be my ticket to paradise. But I had become obsessed with that dream. It affected my judgment in strange ways. It made me impatient, and finally it even made me distrust the advice of my teacher.

The problem was that I began to think I could make things happen more quickly if I moved to the headquarters in Tokyo and trained there. Although Kancho now had his own dojo in Matsuyama, his school was just one of many in the Kyokushin Kai network in Japan and abroad. The top decisions were made at the Tokyo headquarters and the top fighters always seemed to train in Tokyo. Even though Kancho was one of the organization's highest instructors, I was eager to test myself against the best students. More importantly, the fighters who were chosen for America and Europe always came from the Tokyo headquarters. To my nineteen-year-old mind, it only made sense that Tokyo was the place for me to go. I talked several times with Kancho about it, but he told me to wait. He said that I wouldn't be able to find a good teacher in Tokyo, because they were usually transferred out to dojos in other cities to strengthen the network. "Be patient," he insisted.

But Kancho was talking to a wall; my mind was made up. I wrote a note thanking Kancho for his kindness and instruction. I explained that I had thought things over and believed that going to Tokyo was the only way to make my dream come true. I enclosed my black belt and dropped the package by the dojo when Kancho wasn't there.

That night I caught the ferry to Uno and bought a ticket on the midnight train to Tokyo. The train stopped at every station along the way, and I hardly slept a wink. I arrived in Tokyo the next evening and went directly to the main dojo. When I arrived, training had just finished. I was met at the front desk by a Mr. Goda—a kindly older man who treated me very well. He insisted on taking me out to a bath to unwind after my long trip. He asked what had brought me to Tokyo, and as I told him about my desire to go to America, he nodded in a patient manner. Then he calmly talked to me about my decision. He explained how important it was to follow one's teacher. He said he knew Kancho, and believed that if Kancho had told me he intended to send me to America, he undoubtedly would.

His reasons all made good sense. His calm voice and the hot bath relaxed me. Mr. Goda made it sound as if the only reasonable decision was to go back and train with my teacher. We returned to the dojo, and Mr. Goda gave me a bed in the dormitory. I lay down and shut my eyes, but I felt more confused than ever. I tossed and turned, wrestling with my dilemma. Kancho had been the best possible teacher I could find. I kept hearing Mr. Goda's voice: "Your teacher made you who you are. You must follow your teacher." But then, with the next breath, I heard my own impatience calling: "You don't need your teacher. Stay here and you will get to America faster. Hurry, Ninomiya! Hurry!"

As the voices echoed in my head, I drifted in and out of sleep until the the first light of dawn, when I heard still another voice, much closer, calling me from back from my troubled sleep.

"Good morning, Ninomiya."

It was Kancho. He was standing at the foot of my bed. I shook my head, thinking that I was just dreaming.

"I had business in Tokyo," he said. "I thought I would drop by to see how you were doing."

Seeing Kancho suddenly warmed my heart. I felt the depth of his concern for me and for what I was doing with my life. I knew that concern went far beyond the cash he gave me to buy food, the jobs he found for me, or the clothes he passed my way. He knew I needed to feel independent, but he didn't want to see me make a mistake. I knew that's why he was standing in the dormitory waiting for me to clear the sleep from my eyes.

Hadn't he told me about his dream of going to America and how it never came true? Hadn't he told me he could help me? Why had I rejected that help? I suddenly felt very ashamed for running off alone to chase impatiently after my dream. Kancho looked at me with a forgiving expression. He didn't need to say anything. I could still hear his words to me in Yawatahama: "There are ways to make your dream come true. It takes planning and work. We can reach that goal together."

"Kancho," I said. "If you will have me, I would like to come back and start once more as a white belt."

That afternoon I went back to Matsuyama and started training. I lined up with the white belts. I bowed to the upper belts, to whom I had been senpai. After three weeks Kancho gave me back my black belt—a sign that he had forgiven me for having run off. But I hadn't yet forgiven myself for what I had done to him. I wore the black belt, but inside I felt as if I had made a new start. I wanted more than ever to prove myself to Kancho.

My experience in Tokyo helped me to put my dreams in perspective. If I wanted so badly to go to America, I would have to first prove myself in Japan. That meant I would have to do much better in the All-Japan and show that I deserved to go to America.

On November 4, 1973, I fought in my third national tournament. I had been training in karate for almost four years. I had been challenged in the street. I had sought out challenges against other dojos. I felt more prepared than ever before.

In the first round I faced a tall American from Alabama. He had the same build as Jarvis—his upper body was well developed, but his legs were thin and I knew they wouldn't stand up to too many low kicks. This was my first official fight against a foreigner, and I felt that I had something to prove. When we got into the ring, my judgment proved correct; he had fast hands, but he didn't get much weight behind them and his punches lacked power. The fight was soon over. I attacked with a series of low kicks. Finally he went down and couldn't stand up again. The victory felt good. I felt I had partly evened the score for my dismal showing with Jarvis.

The second round fight also went quickly in my favor. When my third round bout came, however, I was matched against Mr. Hatsuo Royama, a strong, very powerful fighter who had trained previously with Kancho. Mr. Royama had been training in karate for ten years and had much more experience than I, but I felt strong and determined to win.

Mr. Royama's fighting style was simple yet effective. Everything came from his right side: he attacked with a right straight punch to the body, followed by a right low kick, and a right *sankaku geri* (triangle kick) to the ribs. Even when I knew the sankaku geri was coming, I couldn't seem to block it in time. Each one slipped under my elbow and rammed into my rib cage. I was able to score with my own techniques, and the match was very close. We fought an overtime period, and Mr. Royama kept coming at me with the same unstoppable combinations. When it was over the referees awarded him the decision. I had finished in the top six, and Mr. Royama went on to win the tournament. Although I was in better physical condition than ever, once again I felt as though I had lost the mental battle. I had pushed myself further, but still not far enough.

I drove myself back into the dojo and vowed that my time would come. A month later, after I had finished training one night, Kancho called me over after class and told me that headquarters had just called. His face was beaming. "They have selected the top fighters to train for the World Tournament next year," he said. "They are sending six of them to New York to train for two months. They want you to go."

I was not yet twenty years old, and my dream of going to America was about to come true. But along with great happiness I also felt anxious about what I would find in America. Finally, there came the evening at Takahama Harbor when Kancho and all of the students from the dojo were standing on the dock saying good-bye to me.

It was a chilly evening, but my eyes were warm as I glanced at the boat and then back at the faces of the other students. I tried to act very self-assured, but Kancho saw through it immediately.

"Ninomiya," he asked, "are you a little nervous?"

I nodded. "It's worse than before the All-Japan."

He put his arm around my shoulders and walked me away from the group. "Don't worry about those giants you'll face in the United States. Just remember: Under the surface, everyone has the same worries and the same doubts as you. We're all only human. Just do your best."

He was wearing a soft beige wool scarf. He took it off and wrapped it around my neck. "I would like for all of us to say 'Banzai!'" he said, "but this is just the beginning for you. When you come back and win the All-Japan, then we'll give you a hero's celebration."

He shook my hand and pulled the scarf snug, like a father sending his son out into the cold. "Try hard in New York," he ordered softly.

I bowed. Then I grabbed my suitcase and ran onto the boat so no one would see my tears.

Three

There were six fighters and one trainer in our group bound for New York. As the top karate students in Japan, we had been hand picked to go to America to train for the First All-World Tournament. For the next two months we would share meals and living quarters. We would work out together at Kyokushin Kai dojos in and around New York, and we would face top American fighters, some of whom were already well known in Japan. For all of us it was the first time abroad, and the long flight gave everyone a chance to get to know one another—everyone, that is, except for me.

While the others forgot about karate for a few hours, loosened their ties, lounged on their seats, and spent the flight sharing backgrounds and stories from home, I sat nervously staring out the window like a wooden doll.

I suppose part of it was that I have always been shy by nature. I don't open up to others easily, and being the youngest fighter in the group—everyone else was five to ten years older than I—made me more self-conscious and also very serious. Then there was the added pressure of being one of the few fighters who hadn't trained at headquarters in Tokyo. I saw myself as Kancho's representative from Matsuyama, and I wanted very much to prove that we

*"Banzai!" as we departed Tokyo's Haneda Airport
for special training in the United States. At nineteen,
I was the youngest in the group. Standing to the right of me,
with his arms raised, is Mas Oyama.*

turned out fighters every bit as good as those from head-quarters. In my own mind I had built up this competition, and even when relaxing with my new friends on the plane, I still felt the keen edge of rivalry pushing between us.

Finally, there was the problem of alcohol; some people could drink the stuff all night, but I couldn't stand even a thimbleful. For some reason the least swallow would make my face red as a beet—my limbs would swell and I would break out in a rash. Until recently, if seniors insisted on buying me drinks, I would take a few swallows to be socia-ble, but anything more played havoc with my system. Lately I have gotten used to drinking a little more because it's important to me to be able to go out and relax with students and friends. But in those days I was almost allergic to alcohol. On the plane to America, while my new friends drank toast after toast and opened their whiskey-lubricated hearts to one another, I sat like a stick, measuring each swallow and trying not to scratch at the rashes breaking out under my shirt.

Before we left, our training group had been nicknamed "The Seven Samurai." We were a mixture of city and farm types from all over Japan. Two of us went on to win All-Japan National Championships, one of us now serves the public as a politician, and almost all the others continue to teach karate. As different as we were, the two-month adventure in America would bring us all close together, and to this day I think of everyone in the group as a friend.

The coach sent to look after us on our trip abroad was none other than Shihan-dai Yuzo Goda, the same gentleman who met me in Tokyo when I ran away from the dojo in Matsuyama the year before. The senior fighter was Senpai Yoshiji Soeno. Next was Senpai Sachio Nishida, who was built like a weight lifter and was doubtlessly the strongest one in our group. Senpai Katsuaki Sato, the tallest, would go on to win two All-Japan Championships. Like myself, Senpai Nobuyuki Kishi came from a farming background. Although the rest of us were to return to Japan after two months, it had already been arranged for Senpai Kishi to stay on to teach in one of the New York branches; of all the fighters in our group, I would develop the closest bond with him. After Senpai Kishi came Senpai Toshikatsu Sato from Akita. In those days, in addition to training in karate, Senpai Sato from Akita also ran a restaurant. When we reached New York, his expertise would come in handy when the job of preparing meals fell to the youngest fighters.

After a ten-hour flight, our plane set down in snow-blanketed Anchorage, Alaska. We all had our first glimpse of the United States, and as we changed planes for our flight to

New York, we couldn't stop talking about the wonderful greeting that probably awaited us there.

Six hours later we made our approach to Kennedy Airport outside of New York. I could see the city laid out below in a perfect grid of streets that extended to the horizon. The miles and miles of square blocks looked like a checkerboard, compared to the random street patterns of our Japanese cities. Excitedly we discussed how many students would be waiting for us at the airport. We each hurried to the bathroom to freshen up and comb our hair. In our anticipation after the long flight, we now expected at least a hundred students from the New York dojos to be lined up in perfect order, eager to greet us as we stepped off the plane.

The plane landed, and as it taxied to the gate we were still busy straightening our ties. Finally we walked out of the exit gate onto the concourse. We each puffed out our chest and lined up in order of seniority, waiting for the senior from the New York dojo to run up and introduce us to his students. We stood and waited. Five, ten, twenty minutes went by. We started to fidget anxiously. There must have been a mistake—no senpai, no teacher. Hundreds of strangers kept pushing by us, staring at us in our bright yellow blazers, all lined up for review like palace guards—but not a soul from the New York dojo.

Two and a half hours later Senpai Kanamura from the Brooklyn dojo arrived and found a tired group of Japanese fighters sitting on their cases in the middle of the floor. When he learned that we had been waiting all that time, he explained that heavy tailwinds must have brought our flight in early. Nobody said anything, but we all knew that only a monsoon could have brought us in that early.

"The important thing is that you're here," Senpai Kanamura said. "Welcome to New York!"

Senpai Kanamura herded us out to the street, where he hailed what looked like a small, dirty yellow truck—an American taxicab. We climbed inside and I sat on a greasy, plastic jump seat facing backward, squeezed shoulder to shoulder with the others, as Senpai Kanamura gave us a quick tour of Brooklyn on the way to our apartment.

Everything felt different—the air was thinner, the houses and cars were larger. The people walking the streets and driving on the expressways had every color of skin and hair imaginable. They seemed to have come from every corner of the globe. After a while my head felt as if were spinning. I don't know whether it was from the newness and vastness of it all or just from riding backwards for so long. Finally Sempai Kanamura stopped the taxi at an old brick building across the street from a large open park. He led us up three flights of stairs to a small apartment that would have comfortably held a couple of pygmies and maybe a pet beetle. And then, happily, he announced: "This is going to be home for the next two months, fellows. Make yourselves comfortable."

Even with the seven of us jammed in like sardines, I couldn't complain about our new quarters. At least it had a toilet and running water. After my apartment in Matsuyama, this little box in Brooklyn felt like the Imperial Palace.

The next morning the alarm went off at 5:00 sharp. At 5:03 I was standing in line waiting to use our apartment's only bathroom. At 5:20 I was still waiting, wondering why it took some of the senpai so long to accomplish the simplest of bodily functions. Maybe it was hard to concentrate with six impatient men waiting on the other side of the door. Maybe it was jet lag. At any rate, I decided that the next morning I would try to sneak in before anyone else. Of course, the following morning everyone else had the same bright idea, and from then on the ten-yard dash for the bathroom was a daily event in which I rarely, if ever, finished in the money. Actually, I think some of the senpai slept with their eyes open, so they could be the first out of bed when the alarm went off. I was amazed at the way they would jump from their beds to the bathroom door like rabbits, only to turn into snails once they got inside.

It was important to get to the bathroom early, because exactly at 5:30 A.M., whether you were ready or not, the group took off for a five-mile run around Prospect Park across the street. It was February, and very cold in New York. After running, we would stay in the park and work out on basics, kata (forms), and techniques. It wasn't hard to keep moving through these chilly workouts; if we didn't, our blood would freeze in our veins. At about eight o'clock the group returned to the apartment. If you were on one of the two-man cooking teams, you had to leave training a half hour early, run back to the apartment, and prepare breakfast.

The four youngest fighters were responsible for preparing all meals, and the two teams took turns on a daily basis. Having lived on a diet of ramen and rice, I had never cooked meat before. On my first few tries I burned it so badly, it tasted like shoe leather. Luckily I had Senpai Sato from Akita as my partner; he taught me how to prepare a few dishes and gradually I became a better cook, although I don't think the group ever thought to present me with any awards.

Usually around one o'clock we set off for one of the dojos in or around Manhattan. We always traveled by subway, and the New York subways were a constant reminder of the vast differences between our cultures. In Japan the subways are a model of social harmony—efficient and clean. In America, however, there isn't nearly the same level of group pride. To put it bluntly, New York subways were the public toilets of mass transportation; the cars were covered with spray-paint graffiti, their floors littered with trash. The stations were dark and dingy, patrolled by policemen with dogs. The passengers were all unfriendly and suspicious. The underground platforms were like hostile stages on which any kind of mishap from robbery to rape could occur, and it wasn't hard to imagine that no one would lift a finger to help the victim. I spent a lot of time on the subways and trains commuting to the various dojos around New York. It made the hair stand up on the back of my neck, and I always rode with one hand glued to my wallet. Nowhere was the cultural gap between Japan and this new land more apparent.

In America, I was also surprised to see so many black faces, especially in the subways. I was unused to being around Afro-Americans, and in the subways I felt a little fearful of them. After growing up in a land where everyone looked and talked the same, I had many prejudices to overcome, but so did the Americans. They may call America a melting pot, but it wasn't long before I discovered how careful Americans were about whom they melted with and how little they knew about Asians. In our Brooklyn neighborhood most of the families were Afro-American, and our group of Japanese fighters stood out. The neighbors were friendly enough, and the kids called us "the karate guys." But then all the Asians in the neighborhood—even those who had never stepped foot into a dojo—were called "karate guys."

There were three Kyokushin Kai dojos in the New York area that we visited on a regular basis: Shihan Oyama's in Scarsdale, Shihan Nakamura's in Manhattan, and Shihan Kanamura's in Brooklyn. Normally we arrived at a dojo by two o'clock in the afternoon and stayed until the dojo closed at nine that evening. At the end of the evening we showered at the dojo before returning to our apartment for dinner. We usually ate dinner at ten, and by the time we cleaned up and were ready for sleep, it was eleven.

At first I had trouble falling asleep. The traffic noises were loud, and the radiator pipes knocked all through the night as if somebody were banging on them with a hammer. At three or four in the morning, the trash collectors arrived, determined, it seemed, to make as much noise as possible. They threw the metal cans around like cymbals, and their compactors roared like bulldozers leveling the street. I was told the trash trucks came in the middle of the night so their trucks wouldn't block the streets during the day. Only in New York are they so considerate that they will keep you up all night so as not to create traffic jams by day.

Like most Japanese, I had studied English in high school and thought I understood enough to get by; I couldn't have been more wrong. Americans spoke much faster than my high school English teacher, and I was constantly mixed up and had to struggle to make myself understood. I had even more trouble trying to understand American money. In fact, on my very first day in America, the money and language nearly defeated me once and for all.

I was sent out to buy toothbrushes and toothpaste. I got to the drugstore, found the items all right, and brought them to the cash register. But when the clerk told me how much it would cost, I was dumbfounded by the strange currency. It didn't make sense; a coin worth one cent was larger than a coin worth ten cents, and a coin worth five cents was larger than both. As the clerk waited for his money, I tried to figure out how much to give him. It was hopeless. I felt a sudden wave of panic. I imagined being cut off from the others, alone in this vast city and hardly able to make myself understood. I felt as though I had been set adrift in a rubber raft in the middle of the ocean. Finally I just thrust out my hand and said, "Please, take it!" The clerk snickered, took some of the bills and coins, and gave me change. I didn't care if it was correct or not. I ran all the way back to the apartment, and when I saw the faces of the other fighters, I felt like embracing each and every one of them. Later on, I just felt embarrassed and small. How could I dream of coming to America and being on my own when I didn't even know how to pay for toothpaste? I had a lot to learn.

The main reason we were sent to America was to prepare for the Kyokushin All-World Tournament by testing our skills against larger fighters. There were several American fighters we were to face who had become well known in Japan. Two of these were William Oliver and Willie Williams. At first I was a little awed by their reputations, but I quickly learned that the image of the fighter and the reality of the man that emerged in kumite could be as different as night and day. The trick was to respond to the man and not his reputation.

As I said, I wanted to prove myself to the others in our group, and I certainly didn't want to lose to an American—none of us did. We took these challenges with deadly seriousness. After all, karate was originally a Japanese martial art, and who should be better at it than the Japanese? The Americans, of course, also felt that they had something to prove; and as a result, whenever we visited a dojo, there was always a great deal of tension in the air. It only got worse. From the very first kumite in the first dojo we visited, there existed an undeclared state of war between the Japanese and American fighters. It was a war that would last for two months.

One of my first skirmishes was against William Oliver in Shihan Nakamura's dojo in Manhattan. At the time, Oliver was the U.S. Lightweight Karate Champion. In Japan I had heard about his lightning-fast kicks, and when he arrived at the dojo I could tell from the way he loosened up before class that he was flexible and extremely quick. I was fascinated by the way he spun and leaped across the floor like a ballet dancer. He put together combinations of kicks and punches with almost invisible speed that made me feel slow as a draft horse. But even more impressive to me were the kiai that came out of his small, black, wiry body. Oliver would growl. He would whine. He would whinny like a horse, shriek like a peacock, and even gobble and cluck. I never heard so many noises coming out of a human being—he sounded like a one-man zoo.

Like most fighters, I didn't like to think about the possibility of losing to someone smaller than I, especially in America where everything was large—the houses, the cars, the people. After all, that's why I had come to New York, to face bigger fighters. I had been looking forward to the challenge of matching my spirit and technique against jumbo fighters, but now, the first fighter I was supposed to face hardly reached my chin. And the thought of losing to him— no matter what his reputation—was like a burr in my side.

Even though Oliver had a formidable reputation and had been fighting against the top fighters in America for several years, I knew that much of his reputation came from victories decided under point-system rules. There is a big difference between a point scored by touch and one scored by the crushing impact of a true punch. As it turned out during kumite, I was used to the contact and Oliver wasn't. His speed was impressive enough, but he lacked power, and when he tried a jump-kick to my stomach, I simply stepped in and pushed him down. His kicks made contact all right, but I hardly felt it. Had he been larger, with more power behind those fancy techniques, William Oliver might have been a tougher opponent. As it was, I had no trouble wading through his leaping kicks and barnyard kiai to bring him down.

Two days later our group took the train to Scarsdale, a suburb of New York, and in the dojo there, at the end of a long series of kumite for both groups, I faced Willie Williams. The fighters in Scarsdale had already heard about our battle in Manhattan, and they were waiting for us, especially Williams, a tall, mean-looking black fighter with braided hair and a fierce kiai that rattled the windows.

As the youngest in our group, I fought last in each round, which allowed me to watch the others closely and figure out which techniques would work best. In the first kumite, one of our senpai faced a tall American fighter. Each time the senpai attacked with a low kick, the American punched him in the chest before the kick even made contact. Three times the American knocked down my senpai, and each time I grew more furious inside. I remembered the humiliating lesson Jarvis had taught me in the dojo at Yawatahama. But I tried to see through that curtain of anger and analyze what was going on. I knew that low kicks would work, but how? Finally I realized that I would have to disguise them; instead of marching in right away with a low kick, I would fake a left-right *nihon-zuki* (double punch) and follow it immediately with a low kick. It worked perfectly. My first opponent was a tall fellow who not only fell for my fakes, but telegraphed his own roundhouse kicks by opening his hips before each one.

After I tagged him with a third low kick, he went down and stayed there.

Next, Senpai Sato from Tokyo faced Willie Williams, and the room went quiet as they squared off in the middle of the floor. They clashed in a flurry of kicks, and each time Senpai Sato punched Williams in the chest, Williams growled, making a fierce face, and charged the senpai like a raging bull. Although Senpai Sato's technique was more polished, they fought evenly. When Senpai Sato finally caught Williams in an *ipponzeoi* (a one-arm judo throw) and threw him over his back, Williams was ready to explode. They were at the point of killing each another when Shihan Oyama called a halt to their kumite.

After Williams caught his breath, it was my turn to face him. He was eager for revenge, and as we squared off he glared down at me impatiently and growled, trying to make me cringe with fear. But I kept looking into his eyes, trying to see behind that mask of ferociousness, and I encountered just what Kancho had told me to expect—a human being. I knew that everyone felt nervous before a fight, and I sensed that Williams was using his growls and nasty faces like a mask to hide behind. There was something almost funny in the way he contorted his face, trying to look so mean, and I had to keep myself from smiling.

Finally he came at me, punching hard to the chest. He had a longer reach than I, and his punches landed like bricks. But I refused to back up. Each punch made me more and more determined. Then I countered, attacking with low kicks and punches. Williams answered with high kicks. Again, I could see those kicks coming early, almost in slow motion. I stopped them easily and countered with a series of faked nihon-zuki (double punches) and hobbling low kicks that landed hard. When Shihan Oyama ordered us to stop, we had finished dead even. Williams didn't know what hit him; he had never seen low kicks combined with punches before. None of the Americans had. Before long, all the students we met in New York, Brooklyn, and Scarsdale were talking about this "new technique" from Japan.

I fought Williams many more times after that. We would often use throwing techniques on each other, but no matter how many times the two of us ended up on the floor, I always wound up on top with Williams pinned beneath me. Shihan Oyama later told me that Williams had come to him one day asking how I managed to pin him each time. When Shihan Oyama told him I had taken six years of judo, Williams just walked off shaking his head.

With each return visit, the war between the Japanese and American fighters intensified. We watched the enemy's every move and talked constantly within our group about the best techniques to use against them. The fighting was wearing on us physically and emotionally, but no matter how bruised and sore we were, we never let it show to the Americans.

At the end of our first month in New York, a teaching job at Shihan Oyama's dojo in Scarsdale became available, and he offered me the opening. I jumped at the chance to stay on in America and make my dream come true, but some of the others in our group saw it differently. Senpai Sato from Tokyo, for one, sat me down and said, "*Ninomiya-kun* [a diminutive that expresses affection], if you go to teach in Scarsdale, you'll have to fight them every day . . . you'll get killed. I wouldn't be so eager to go up there full-time if I were you."

But my mind was made up. I didn't care how tough the fighters were. I called Kancho to ask his permission to stay, and he said Shihan Oyama had already called to explain the opening at his dojo. Kancho told me he thought I was still too young. My heart dropped, but before I could say anything, Kancho added that he thought it would be a good opportunity for me. I could stay, he said, but I would have to keep training hard. "*Osu*," I said—a dojo expression meaning "Yes, I'll keep trying." He kept talking, giving me further instructions, but I hardly heard them. "Osu!" It was a good thing Kancho couldn't see me right then, because I couldn't stop jumping up and down. "Osu . . . osu!" I shouted. "Osu!" I must have sounded like a whistling kettle.

At the end of March, the "war" in New York was over for most of our group. It was time for our fighters to return home, and Senpai Kishi and I went along to the airport to see them off. For the past two months these men had given me much support and encouragement. The senpai had taught me many things about karate and life. It had seemed like such a long time together. As we shook hands and said goodbye, they told me to be strong and try hard. "See you next tournament," they said.

Senpai Kishi and I watched their plane taxi away from the gate, and when they were out of sight, we caught a train back into the city. Riding along in the noisy subway car, I closed my eyes and suddenly felt very alone inside. By staying in America, I had sealed my fate. My life was about to unfold in a new direction and yet I couldn't see exactly what lay ahead.

"Be strong. Try hard. . . ." The words rang in my ears along with the roar of the train rushing through the tunnel. I looked over at Senpai Kishi. He smiled at me reassuringly. We had become good friends, and together we were on our way back to an apartment that we would share in Manhattan. Plunging through the dark subway tunnel into an unknown future, I worried about just where that journey would take me, but I was comforted to know I would have the guidance of Senpai Kishi along the way.

During my first two months in New York, aside from learning how to get along in a strange country, I had been concerned only with proving myself as a fighter. Since the age of seventeen, I had geared my entire life toward training for the rigors of the All-Japan competition, and I had thought about little else. Once I moved in with Senpai Kishi, however, a different world opened up for me. I had certainly heard of bushido—the samurai warrior's code—but I never fully understood its significance. With Senpai Kishi, I would begin to learn about the samurai spirit and the inner world of *karate-do*.

Senpai Kishi was six years older than I. He had grown up on a farm in Yamagata, where he was the older of two brothers. When he came to the United States with our group of Japanese fighters, he expected to be in New York for only three years before returning home to take care of his family. That was in 1974; today he still lives in Manhattan and is still more dedicated to his art than almost any *karateka* (karate practitioner) I have ever met.

Senpai Kishi started training in karate at the age of eighteen, when he moved to Tokyo. His first day in the dojo he was so badly beaten up by the senpai that he considered giving up the whole idea right then and there. But he decided that if he quit, he would remain a quitter for the rest of his life. So he forced himself back into the dojo. He took the lumps and bruises until he learned how to answer the blows from the senpai. Once he had learned how to defend himself, he began to delve into the deeper secrets that karate had to offer—secrets about the mind and spirit. Karate had given a purpose and direction to his life, and he vowed never to forget that purpose.

Senpai Kishi and I shared a sixth-floor walk-up apartment in Greenwich Village, across the street from Washington Square Park. The ceiling plaster dropped in huge chunks, and the linoleum flooring curled at the walls. We slept on tumbling mats and ate at a metal table whose legs were held together with pieces of rope. None of this bothered Senpai Kishi. He liked the challenge of hardship to test his spirit. He considered the purpose of life to reach beyond the limits of the mind, to remake the inner man, to adapt to any hardship. In Senpai Kishi, I saw a man who lived the principles of *budo* day to day.

Running through the streets of Manhattan with my good friend and mentor, Sensei Nobuyuki Kishi (far left).

One afternoon in our apartment, Senpai Kishi was lying on his mat, propped on one elbow, addressing me as I stood in the doorway. "Everyone today forgets the challenge of bushido," he said. "They only want money. And once they get money, they forget about karate." Just then the ceiling rumbled, and a large chunk of plaster broke loose, falling with a crash to the mat where Senpai Kishi was lying. Catlike, he had sprung out of the way and calmly went on speaking as though nothing had happened. "If things are easy, you forget your purpose. You lose your way. And when you lose your way, you lose your spirit when the least struggle arises."

I once heard about Senpai Kishi's legendary spirit from two friends of his—a judo player and a painter—who were present at a demonstration where Senpai Kishi had attempted to break a baseball bat with a shin strike. There are two types of baseball bats—hard and soft wood—and most karateka use the softer bat for breaking demonstrations. Senpai Kishi, however, insisted on challenging himself to break a hardwood bat. He had seen a commercial on television advertising an unbreakable wooden bat, and that was the one against which he was determined to test himself. He prepared himself and finally struck the bat with a devastating shin strike. But the bat didn't yield. Again he prepared himself and struck the bat with his shin, but again it didn't break. The third time he poured every ounce of effort and power into an awesome shin strike that easily would have broken two normal bats. Still the bat wouldn't break. Calmly, without a word, Senpai Kishi walked away and sat down at the side of the room as if nothing had happened.

When the judo player and painter went over to console their friend, they found him hunched over attending to his shin. Suddenly they noticed his leg was bent at a sickening angle; he had broken it at the shin. With superhuman effort, he was attempting to set the leg straight with his own hands and tie it in place with a belt. "Are you all right?" they cried. Senpai Kishi shook his head. "The angle," he said. "The angle of the kick was all wrong." In spite of having badly broken his leg, Senpai Kishi was still concentrating on the baseball bat. It wasn't until eleven-thirty that night, when he agreed to go to the hospital to have the leg set in a cast, that Senpai Kishi admitted how painful his injury had been. Typically, in the spirit of budo, he had not expressed his feelings in public. He had remained concentrated on the challenge before him and had totally accepted the consequences of that challenge.

Many of the books one sees these days extol the virtues of budo. And yet many of the writers who tell us to purify our spirits and concentrate only on budo seem more interested in making money than in following the true spirit of the samurai. Senpai Kishi is different. In an age when billboards, radio, and TV constantly urge us to acquire more and more material possessions, Senpai Kishi still lives simply like the samurai of three hundred years ago. He gives no thought to money, success, or fame. During the week he teaches in a walk-up dojo in Manhattan, and on weekends he travels to a cottage in the country that he has built by hand. It is located on a few acres of land that his students gave to him as an expression of their affection. There he meditates and carves *bokuto* (wooden swords).

Like a modern day Mushashi, Senpai Kishi has been a spiritual beacon marking the way I have chosen. I sometimes wish Senpai Kishi would find the recognition I feel he deserves. And yet I know that even if it were to come, he would reject it, insisting instead that his way has provided its own rewards.

The four months Senpai Kishi and I shared our Greenwich Village apartment was a special period in my life, but a very exhausting one as well. The long hours commuting back and forth to Scarsdale by train each day began to wear on me. I had to leave the apartment early each morning and didn't get back until almost midnight. Finally I took an apartment in Scarsdale. My routine became less hectic, and though I didn't get to see Senpai Kishi as often, we sometimes spent a Sunday together just talking.

I continued to train every day and split my teaching time between the Scarsdale and Fairfield, Connecticut, dojos. Because of "green card" complications, I couldn't go home to fight in the 1974 All-Japan tournament, and after having trained hard for a whole year I felt as though the rug had been pulled out from under me. It would have been easy to feel sorry for myself, to think of the whole year as a waste of time. But I knew I was stronger. I knew my technique was better. It was time to look ahead, not backward. Besides, there was nothing I could do to change my work status. Anyone who has come to the United States and run through the "green card" maze knows how important it is not to create problems. As it turned out, the First All-World Tournament was pushed back a year. So I continued training with my sights now set on 1975.

In Fairfield I was working out with Willie Williams and two friends of his, Frank Clark and a fellow whom I can only recall as Gary. The three of them were also training for the world tournament, and each week they drove six hours from the northern end of New York state to meet me in Fairfield. We would train together during the afternoon; then they would stay overnight and drive back the next day.

Once the "war" in New York had ended and the other Japanese fighters had gone home, I began to discover a warm, friendly man behind Willie Williams's intimidating mask. Frank Clark, who was Williams' best friend, had trained previously as a boxer. Together, the four of us pushed ourselves to the limit as Shihan Oyama hovered over us with a *shinai*—a bamboo sword—and lashed our thighs at the slightest letdown. No matter how hard we hit the heavy bag, our shihan was dissatisfied, and he would show that dissatisfaction by wearing out one shinai each month.

When I moved to Scarsdale, I was put in charge of the dojo there. I lived across the street from the dojo and shared a very pleasant apartment with a green belt named Ralph Rhoads, who was five years older than I. Ralph had a generous spirit and helped me enormously through the transition of moving out from Manhattan. Today Ralph is still a close friend. He lives in California, where he is a marketing specialist and runs an Enshin dojo in San Rafael.

Running a dojo for the first time, I was eager to make a good impression on the students there. At first many of the students stayed away, probably waiting to see how I would fill in as the shihan's replacement. But I didn't like the idea of teaching to a half-empty dojo, and to get the students back I felt I had to do something to prove myself. So, each night at the end of class, I started sparring with every student in the dojo. It was an exhausting workout, but I knew it would be good preparation for the tournament. Even better, the students loved it. I controlled my kicks and punches, and the sparring gave them a regular opportunity to sharpen their technique. After a few weeks more and more students began showing up for evening class. The extra workout helped so much that I kept on doing it every night.

Teaching on my own for the first time, I was able to take some of the values I had learned from Kancho and Senpai Kishi and use them in my own classes. It was gratifying to see the positive changes that began to appear in my students. As a result, I began to think more and more about teaching and one day having my own dojo.

In Scarsdale there were three students in particular with whom I began to train on a regular basis; over the next few years we developed a special relationship. Greg Vahenian, Humberto Leon, and Vernon Brown were all only thirteen or fourteen years old when they started training with me at the Scarsdale dojo. The day they started, they were just three kids looking in the window as I pounded the heavy bag inside. When I jogged outside onto Central Avenue, the main street of Scarsdale, I waved for them to follow me. They fell in behind me and kept on following me for the next three years. When I moved to Colorado, they even followed me out there and helped me to set up my new dojo. Some students a teacher never forgets. I think Vahenian, Leon, and Brown will always be special in my memory. They were the first group of students that I personally trained all the way to black belt.

Recently I saw Vahenian in New York, and he thanked me for the six years he had spent training in karate. He said it had given structure to what had been a difficult time in his life. Vahenian was later in an auto accident that injured his neck and back, forcing him to stop training. He studied to be an actor, and explained to me that the discipline and spirit he developed in karate had carried over into this new aspect of his life as well. As a teacher, it heartened me to see how my student had carried karate out of the dojo and adapted its principles to a different part of his life.

During that first year in New York, I was slowly making a similar transition for myself. I had been training in the martial arts since the age of fifteen, and much of that time I had spent in the dojo mastering techniques. In New York I felt for the first time some profound changes stirring inside me. In karate I started searching for something more than physical strength and technical perfection. I was entering another difficult period of doubt and frustration, in which my patience and will would be tested to their limits. The path of karate was turning steeper and more perilous, and it would be some time before it was clear to me just what kind of changes that journey was affecting within me. But I would not give in, and I would not give up my search.

In late October of 1975 I returned to Japan for the First All-World Tournament held in the Tokyo Gymnasium. The tournament hosted 128 of the top fighters from more than thirty different countries. When I flew back with Senpai Kishi and several others who would be representing Japan in the tournament, I was twenty-one years old, and I had been out of the country for almost two years. Because the world tournament was being hosted by Japan, there was naturally a lot of pressure on me and the other Japanese fighters to do well. I didn't mind the pressure. I was looking forward to the challenge, and after having trained every day for the last two years, I felt I was truly prepared both mentally and physically.

I arrived in Tokyo a week early and stayed with my brother Norinaga. I worked out daily on the roof of his apartment building. We rolled up an old futon (a cotton mattress), wrapped it with tape, and hung the makeshift punching bag from a laundry pole. When my brother came home from work, he held armguards for me, which we had fashioned out of pillows tied up with belts.

Three days before the tournament I was working out alone on the roof. I jumped up and grabbed the crossbar of the laundry pole with both hands. I dipped down and was about to begin a series of chin-ups, when something snapped. Pain shot down into my lower back and hips. I couldn't move. I hung from the bar, helpless. Then, slowly, I pulled myself hand-over-hand to the center pole. I slid down the pole and tried to straighten up. Again the pain paralyzed me. I could barely walk; I felt crushed. I had put in two years of training, there were three days left until the tournament, and suddenly I was a cripple.

When my brother arrived home that evening and found me collapsed on the couch, he rushed me to an acupuncturist. After that he took me for *shiatsu* (finger pressure massage). The combination of the two returned movement to my lower back and legs, but I was still in a great deal of pain.

The next day, when Kancho arrived in Tokyo, I didn't mention my back injury to him. We both already had enough to think about, and I wanted to put the injury out of my mind. It felt good to be reunited with my teacher. We had a lot to catch up on, and in between our long talks I continued with light workouts. Two nights before the start of the tournament, I moved into Kancho's hotel room. He continued to ply me with plenty of encouragement and advice. During the tournament his help would prove invaluable. We would huddle between matches down in the warm-up room under the gym, where we talked strategy and analyzed the styles of upcoming opponents.

My brother Norinaga encouraged me to train in karate
and even helped pay for my early lessons. I stayed
with him before the World Tournament in 1975.

My parents came to Tokyo to watch me fight
in the 1975 World Tournament.

My family also arrived just before the start of the tournament, and my father was so excited he didn't stop giving me directions. I told him I already had one coach, but he couldn't control himself. After my first fight he even came down out of the stands and followed me into the bathroom stall. Fortunately, my mother found out and later had a long talk with him. She was able to keep him in his seat during the rest of the tournament.

In the first round I faced a kung fu champion from Hong Kong named Chunning. The press had built up the kung fu challenge to karate, but as it turned out there really wasn't much of a contest. Chunning came straight at me with a series of punches. I stepped outside and countered with a right low kick and a left uppercut to the body. He doubled over and couldn't breathe. They had to stop the fight and awarded me the victory.

During the match I had hardly noticed the pain in my lower back. But down in the warm-up room as I loosened up for my next fight, I had to be careful not to strain it.

In my second-round match, I faced a fighter from Malaysia and won easily. In the third round I stopped Robert Romigo from Argentina with low kick-high kick combinations. The second time that I connected, he went down and stayed there.

My fourth-round match started the next morning at ten o'clock. I faced a Swede named Friebert, whom I knocked down and defeated on points.

In the fifth round, I was slated to fight Mr. Takashi Azuma. Although he was older than I, I was still his senpai and I was confident that I could beat him. I had fought Azuma before in the United States, where he had been part of a training group visiting New York earlier that year. We had faced one another during kumite at the Fairfield dojo. At the time Azuma had a very strong low kick but little else. As I thought out my strategy in the warm-up room, I knew that Azuma would probably come after me with his low kicks. I also knew it would make my job easier if he did. Let me explain.

*My introduction on the second day at 1975 World Tournament.
There were 32 fighters remaining from the original field of 128.*

One of the hardest parts of kumite is figuring out your opponent's strategy and adjusting your own to take advantage of his weaknesses. If your opponent is a one-dimensional fighter who uses the same techniques over and over, it removes the element of surprise. Although it's important to have one technique that is your strongest—that you can rely on when things are tough to pull you through again and again—it's better to be able to show an opponent a variety of techniques in order to keep him off balance. I've always believed that if you can create the element of surprise that comes from mixing your strongest technique with a variety of others, it will make that one strongest technique even more effective.

When I faced Azuma, he came at me, as I expected, with a series of low kicks. I stopped them with my shin, stepped outside, and countered with punches. I also reached him with several roundhouse kicks to the face. Although I didn't knock Azuma down, I clearly dominated, and the referees gave me the decision.

My sixth match was the semifinal round, and it was the contest I had been waiting for: I was to face Senpai Katsuaki Sato, to whom I had lost in overtime in 1971 and who would twice win the All-Japan. I was grateful for the chance again to show my skills against one of the best fighters in the world.

The fight started with us trading punches at close range. When Sato made distance and tried to throw a left round-house kick, I immediately attacked his supporting foot with a sweep. The timing was perfect. He went down and I immediately followed up with a controlled punch. The referees awarded me the first half-point. After that Mr. Sato was in a hurry to even the score. He rushed at me with a flurry of punches and knee kicks. I countered with my own combinations and we continued to fight evenly. As time ran out at the end of the first round, I caught a left mawashi geri to the face. I didn't go down but the referees still awarded a half-point to Mr. Sato.

In the first overtime we again fought evenly. Mr. Sato tried to use his weight advantage and continued to hammer my body with knee kicks and punches. But at the end of the first overtime, no further points had been scored and we were still even.

The second overtime started, and Mr. Sato tried to throw me by using the same ipponzeoi I had seen him use against Willie Williams during their kumite in Scarsdale. I saw it coming, and as he began to lift me, I wriggled free like an eel. When I regained my feet I attacked again, and we continued to fight in close, battering each other with punches to the body.

Remarkably, the referees ordered a third overtime. The audience was excited beyond belief. I felt no fatigue, neither mentally nor physically, and I gave no thought whatsoever to letting down. The past two years of training and kumite had brought me to a level of mental conditioning that would never allow me to consider giving up—I could have fought all afternoon. As for my back, I was too excited to think about the pain.

In the third overtime the battle continued to rage. We tried to wear each other down, and we varied our techniques, hoping to catch each other off guard. I admired Mr. Sato's experience; it enabled him to adapt quickly to whatever I threw at him. The momentum surged back and forth, each of us refusing to give up. Finally, the drum boomed and the match had ended. The crowd was on its feet. The referees conferred and narrowly awarded Mr. Sato the victory. I had nothing to be ashamed of. It had been the best fight of my career, but still I wasn't satisfied.

Mr. Sato went on to defeat Mr. Royama and won the First All-World Tournament. I was supposed to face the loser of the other semifinal round, Mr. Daigo Oishi, in order to determine who would take third place. But Mr. Oishi had been hurt in his semifinal match and had to forfeit his fight with me. I was awarded third place and stood on the awards platform with the other two fighters.

My family was proud of my achievement: I was twenty-one years old and had taken third place in the First All-World Tournament. Kancho shook my hand. He had seen what his student could do, but I knew he would not express his complete approval until I had shown my full potential and taken first place. Everyone seemed satisfied, for now, but me. A loss was a loss, whether it happened in the first round or the final round of a tournament. Third place . . . second place . . .

Landing a roundhouse kick against Mr. Sato in our semifinal round match of the 1975 World Tournament. I scored a half-point takedown against Mr. Sato, and he came back to tie the score. After three overtimes, Mr. Sato was awarded the match on a judges' decision.

With my third place trophy at the end of the 1975 World Tournament.

it didn't matter. I courteously accepted my trophy, but inside I was bitter and disappointed because I hadn't won it all.

The sportswriters declared that my match with Mr. Sato had been the best fight of the tournament. I felt that I had come as close to winning as one possibly could. I had almost tasted the thrill of victory, but once again it had eluded me. Now I wanted the All-Japan more than ever, and that desire tightened something in the pit of my stomach. It locked my senses, mind, and spirit to the achievement of that one goal. No matter what obstacle stood in the way, I would not be denied. I vowed to win the All-Japan or die trying.

When I returned to New York, the students at the Scarsdale dojo threw a large party to celebrate my third place finish. They presented me with a clock mounted on a plaque with an inscription. If I could have turned the hands of that clock forward to the next tournament, I would have done it in a second. As it was, I would have to train for another year before I would have my chance at a championship trophy.

As close as I thought I had come to winning, my friend Senpai Kishi brought me back to reality that evening. He had come from New York for the party and had been quietly watching the celebration from a corner of the room. After an hour or so he took me aside and told me that my fight, in fact, wasn't nearly as close as I had thought. "And what's more," he added, "it's probably a good thing you didn't win."

I couldn't believe my ears. "Why?" I stammered.

"Because if you had won at your age, you would now have nowhere to go. There would be nothing left to challenge you. You would be a precocious champion with all of the outer skills but very few of the inner qualities."

It hurt me to think that my friend was glad I had lost. I was confused, yet as I thought about what he said and remembered the frustration I had felt after losing—my impatience and anger—I realized that he was right. I was thinking only about winning a tournament. I had narrowed my vision to a single trophy. Had I won, it would have been too soon for me. I would have continued to wander through life with my gaze fixed on that one trophy, to the exclusion of everything else.

The next day I started back on my training routine. After my talk with Senpai Kishi, my eyes were open a little wider, and after the long flight back and several days of inactivity, my body was begging for exercise. It felt good to get back into the dojo. Training was never a chore for me. I always thought of each session as a chance to think ahead to the next tournament and reaffirm my goal. I wanted the All-Japan not just for myself. I wanted it especially for Kancho—as a way of repaying him for all his support over the years.

The act of training on a daily basis had become a necessity for me. It provided a purpose to each day. Without a daily workout, I sometimes felt lost and unfocused. Rain, snow, sunshine . . . it didn't matter. I've always felt that it was important to train in all kinds of conditions. In some ways, when the weather was bad, I felt more excited about the challenge of going out to train. If it were raining, I said to myself, "You're going to get wet anyway when you come in to shower. What's the difference if it's now or later?"

Running, frog-jumps, push-ups, sit-ups . . . these were always part of my daily routine. Each week I would try to increase my goal. If I were doing 100 push-ups, I would try to do 105 the following week. I frog-jumped around the perimeter of a parking lot behind an office building on Central Ave. If I had made three trips around the lot and my legs were tired, I would try to push myself the width of one more parking space. I would do this for a week and then increase that distance by one more parking space the next week. I was always trying to challenge myself to do a little more. This is one of the things I had learned from Kancho: "Never stay at the same level of training. Always push yourself to do a little more."

Even if I had an injury, I would go out to train every day. If my leg was sore, I would do extra work on my punches; if my hand was injured, I would work extra on my kicks. There was always something to do to improve my strength or technique.

No matter how hard I trained for the All-Japan, I always told myself there was someone, somewhere, training harder than I; and that thought drove me to keep improving for the day I'd face that fighter. I kept pushing myself this way because I knew that the day I started believing my training was harder than anyone else's would be the day I stopped improving. Training was like climbing a mountain: I wanted to be able to see the top, but I never wanted to reach it. Because the moment I reached the top and stopped to enjoy the view, that's when I would stop climbing. That's the moment the challenge would end.

When I returned to Tokyo for the 1976 All-Japan, I was in top fighting condition and determined to take the title that had eluded me the year before. I didn't know it yet, but I was about to find out how close I could come to capturing my dream, only to have it melt from my exhausted grasp in a final disappointing round.

The first three rounds of the tournament passed without any problems. I easily won each of my matches. In the fourth round, however, I faced Mr. Keiji Sanpei, a twenty-one-year-old brown belt from Hukushima. He was one year younger than I and already a very tough competitor. When I retired in 1978, Mr. Sanpei would go on to take three consecutive All-Japan titles.

Mr. Sanpei had a tough, brawling style, and from the opening drum he came after me with a barrage of punches that wouldn't stop. In the first round, he tore the gi off my back. We went on to fight three grueling overtimes. Both of us refused to quit, and when it was over, the referees awarded me the decision. It was a gratifying victory, but not without its price: Mr. Sanpei had worn me down for my semifinal fight against Mr. Azuma. Even if I got past Mr. Azuma, how much would I have left for the final? I couldn't think about it. I had to give each match everything I had.

Azuma didn't waste any time. He attacked with a steady bombardment of low kicks, and I sensed that he was determined to avenge his loss to me the year before. Having beaten him once already, I felt confident that I could do it again— but I knew it wouldn't be easy.

After two overtimes, I came away with the victory. I had fought two long, grueling matches, and I now had ten minutes to regain my strength for the final. On my way back to my locker room, I glimpsed Mr. Sato from Akita behind the partition in the next room. He was resting, waiting for me.

I collapsed on the training table while five *kohai* (lower belts) furiously massaged my arms and legs, trying to keep me loose. I gobbled four or five lemons to build my strength back. Kancho walked in and asked how I felt. I nodded that I was ready, but he took one look at the sweat pouring off me and said, "I have to go back out. I'm supposed to do a knife throwing demonstration. It might take longer than I planned. . . ."

As the kohai worked over my back and legs, I closed my eyes. I could hear the thunk of Kancho's knives against the wooden targets and the applause of the crowd. I tried to concentrate on Mr. Sato. I remembered last year's tournament. I thought back to our kumite in the dojos around New York, and I planned my strategy. I could have used an hour more to rest, but the announcer's voice suddenly crackled over the loudspeaker, announcing the final match. I heard my name. It was time.

From the opening drum I was slow. My arms were weary. Every punch I threw, it seemed, was countered by Mr. Sato before I could straighten my arm. It was over very quickly. I lost and had to settle for second place. For the second time in two years I had come tantalizingly close to reaching my goal. The taste of defeat was as bitter as a mouthful of ashes.

I had no excuses. Spirit, stamina, technique—it all had to be the best for every round of a tournament. Second place only meant that one of those qualities was not strong enough. I felt that I had reached a turn on the side of the mountain I had been climbing for the last eight years. There was a view of its snow-covered peak, and Mr. Sato of Akita was alone on top. As I stood on the second place level of the awards platform, that peak looked farther away than ever.

Of course I didn't show it on that platform, but inside I felt as if I had hit rock bottom. I could hear Senpai Kishi's words: "Had you won, the challenge would have ended for you. There would have been nothing left for you to strive for."

"What a lot of nonsense!" I thought. Senpai Kishi and his budo could all take a flying leap, for all I cared. I would have gladly taken the first place trophy and gone my way. What did I need with inner struggle? How many more years of training and pushing myself could I endure? How long could I keep working only to have victory keep slipping through my fingers?

But then another voice inside, a calmer voice, took over. It told me there was more to the effort than a gold-plated trophy. There were other rewards. I saw Kancho's patient, knowing stare. He was looking deep inside me, as if at some reservoir filled with a shining essence. What could he see there that I couldn't see for myself? "Be strong. Try hard. . . ."

No, I would not give up. I would not let down until I had reached that snow-covered peak. I would continue to pour my whole life into climbing that mountain, training for this one event and the day when, like Mr. Sato, I would reach the top. In a few days I would return to America and the routine would begin all over.

It was May, a warm, overcast afternoon, and rain was threatening to fall any moment. I was in Senpai Kanamura's dojo in Brooklyn. I was wielding a 350-year-old samurai sword that Shihan Kanamura had given me one day as I admired his extensive collection. He had told me to keep it to use in demonstrations. The scabbard was an old painted wooden case, probably just as old as the sword itself, and the top lip of the scabbard had been split from years of drawing the sharpened blade. The case needed repairing but I had kept putting off the job.

I was preparing to assist Senpai Kanamura in a demonstration that would take place at Madison Square Garden during an upcoming tournament. He was preparing to show barehanded techniques against a sword, and we had been practicing for the last hour. There were only three days left, but the timing of the routine was coming together nicely. "Let's try it one more time," Senpai Kanamura said.

We worked smoothly through five of the techniques, with only one left to finish out the routine. It called for a *nukiuchi*, a movement in which I would draw the sword and simultaneously strike down at Senpai Kanamura's head. He would stop the sword by closing his palms against the sides of the blade at the very last instant. We never got that far.

I gripped the case with my left hand, took the sword handle in my right, and without hesitating drew the razor-sharp blade from the case. Just then a numbness tingled in my left thumb. I looked down at my hand and saw blood squirting in a thin, arcing jet seven feet across the white mats. The top knuckle of my left thumb was bent backward at a queer angle, like an open gate with the blood pouring through.

The blade had cut through the tendon, carving between the bones at the knuckle joint. There was nothing left to keep the thumb in place. The little fountain of blood kept pumping eerily in time to my heartbeat. I pushed the flapping joint back against the base of my thumb and held it there while Sempai Kanamura wrapped it in a towel and rushed me to the hospital.

At the hospital they told me I had cut the nerves as well as the tendons. One of the students from the dojo had contacted the best hand specialist in New York. The tendons and nerves, he explained, had both been cut like rubber bands. Once they were severed, they had snapped back into the base of my thumb. It was going to take special surgery to open the palm, retrieve the severed nerves and tendons, and reconnect them with those in my knuckle. "You may never use the thumb again," he warned.

The operation was performed, and I spent five days in the hospital. The doctor told me that I wouldn't be able to move the thumb for at least three months. I was simply hoping that I hadn't lost the use of my thumb for good. If I had, it would mean the end of my career.

In karate my left hand is particularly important. I not only use it to block and parry, it is an antenna that warns me of my opponent's every move. I could change my style to fight with my right foot and right hand forward, but it would take a long time to get used to it and to perform anywhere near as well as I did the old way. I can't describe the fear and disappointment I felt. The ashen taste of defeat was becoming a regular part of my diet. Still, I refused to give in to it.

Three months after the operation, I could start rehabilitating my hand. I squeezed a rubber ball to rebuild the strength in my thumb. During training I had to wrap the whole hand to keep the thumb from sticking out. The joint was sensitive to the slightest impact, and when I tried sparring with it, the least contact would send a jolt through my arm like an electric shock.

That year's All-Japan was out of the question for me, and it took a long time for me to accept that. I had been hoping against hope that some miracle would happen and I would recover very quickly. But there were no miracles. The tournament would still be there next year, I reasoned. I would take my time, rehabilitate the thumb, and push myself back into peak condition. I didn't want to attempt the All-Japan unless I was in top form. Once again I would have to wait to realize my dream.

Those five days I was laid up in the hospital gave me plenty of time to think. I had been dreaming more and more of having my own school. New York, Chicago, and Los Angeles—these cities were full of karate schools. I wanted to be on my own, and I wanted to move to a town where there weren't as many schools. I would move west, maybe to

Denver—to the Rocky Mountains and the open spaces that had captivated my imagination back in Japan. I had been in New York for three years, and now I had run into some bad luck. That sword had cut more than the tendons in my thumb; maybe it had also cut some of the bonds that tied me to New York. It was time to move on.

By June, I had made up my mind—Denver would be my next home. When I told Shihan Oyama that I would be leaving, he told me I was making a mistake. He said it would be too difficult for me to start a dojo in a city where there was no one to help, and that I would be all alone. But that was exactly what I wanted. As a boy, I had dreamed of leaving Japan to escape the group and test myself alone. In many ways, I always carried with me those few days of solitude on Kawanohama Beach. I never forgot the sense of self-sufficiency I learned there. I would always cherish the ability to look into myself without needing anyone to stare over my shoulder. I wanted my own dojo, but I didn't want teachers in New York or an organization in Tokyo plotting every step of the way for me. If I made mistakes—and I knew I would—they would be my own. I wanted freedom and responsibility and had left Japan to look for both; if I had to travel another two thousand miles from New York to keep searching, so be it. I was determined to make this happen. When I told Kancho, he said he thought it would be a good idea for me to be on my own.

On July 2, I left New York. That night Vahenian, Brown, and Leon threw a going-away party for me, along with the other students at the dojo. It was a sad occasion, but we put on happy faces and tried to lift each other's spirits. Finally it was time to leave. My car was packed and everyone came out to the curb to see me off. My three top students gathered around me. "We want to follow you to Denver," they insisted.

I shook my head sadly. "Not now. One day we'll be together again," I promised. "There will come a time when I need your help setting up a new dojo." Our eyes were moist. There was nothing else to say. We shook hands and I drove off.

I tried not to think of how much I would miss these students who had become close friends. I was turning away from New York, and I couldn't look back. Then I remembered a song that Senpai Kishi had taught me: "Sakura Bana." Its lyrics urged the seeker to live life to the fullest, no matter what may come, just the way the cherry blossom would bloom and fall at the moment of its most exquisite beauty. On the drive across the country, I would keep singing this song, sometimes at a whisper, sometimes at the top of my lungs. It became an anthem for me that gave me strength and renewed my spirit.

Two days later, I arrived in Chicago under a sky full of exploding fireworks. It was American Independence Day— the Fourth of July. Now that I was on my way to a new life, I felt as if I were celebrating my own independence too.

The next morning I drove on, and for the next two days I ploughed my way through the flat Midwestern plains in ninety-degree heat. Miles and miles of endless farmland, corn, and wheat. Then, finally, on the afternoon of the fourth day, I came over a long hill in eastern Colorado and saw the snow-capped Rockies shimmering in the distance. My heart leaped.

I felt as if I had finally discovered paradise—a landscape made for dreams like mine. From north to south, as far as I could see, the mountains hovered majestically under a deep blue sky. After another hour of driving, I could see a city sparkling in the haze—Denver! This was where I would make my mark. This was where I would bury my bones. This was where the cherry blossom would fall. This was one place where, when people heard the word karate, they would think of Joko Ninomiya.

An hour later I was driving along the crowded streets of downtown Denver. Paradise looked much different up close. With the bright glare of chrome and glass in my eyes, horns honking and radios blaring, I tried to get my bearings. I didn't know a soul. I had no place to stay. The bloom was off the cherry blossom, and the challenge was just beginning all over again.

Four

I found an apartment near the center of town, located across the street from a storefront health club. I wasn't looking for a health club when I took the apartment. I didn't even notice the place when I first moved in, but that health club would later turn out to be a lucky find. In the meantime, I was eager to be moving my muscles again. I wanted people to know I was there, to sit up and take notice. I went out for a jog and discovered a small park not five minutes from my apartment building. I went back each afternoon and brought along my heavy bag. I hung it by a rope from one of the tall elms and hammered it with punches and kicks. It was my way of hanging out a sign saying, "Open for business." I was looking for students the same way Kancho told me that he had hung his heavy bag on a telephone pole when he first arrived in Yawatahama.

No matter how overwhelmed I felt by the strange city and the task of starting my own school, my workouts in the park always helped to settle my mind. As I worked on the heavy bag, I would imagine an opponent driving at me with kicks and punches. I would step to the side and counter with combinations of my own. If there were the least hitch or loss of balance, I would do that particular technique again until I had done it perfectly ten times in a row. Before long the sweat would gather on my brow, and my breath would release in soft kiai as my punches and kicks made the bag jump. I was moving to a familiar rhythm that made me feel at home again, like a fish back in its own waters. Sometimes that rhythm would carry me away, all the way back to the dojo at Yawatahama with Kancho carefully watching my every move.

It wasn't long before my workouts started catching the eyes of curious joggers and sunbathers. When they asked what I was training for, I told them about the All-Japan and explained that I had just moved to town. When they asked where I taught, I said that I was planning to open a school in just a few weeks. Some of them were very interested and wanted to start training with me right away. "It won't be long," I promised. . . . All I needed now was a dojo.

After a week in my new apartment, I finally became curious about the health club across the street. One morning I went to have a look for myself, to see what it was all about. I walked into a large, low room arrayed with exercise equipment, free weights, and a heavy bag tucked in the corner. In front, near the large window facing the street, was a fairly large space that seemed unused—it was the perfect size for teaching karate. I kept circling through the health club wondering how I would ever talk the manager into letting me have that space for karate. Just when it seemed pretty hopeless, I spotted an older Japanese man working with barbells in the back corner.

I went over and introduced myself. He said his name was Tony Hamada and told me that he came to the club to work out every day. He looked it. He was a tall, big-shouldered fellow who hardly looked his sixty years. Although he had been born and raised in Hawaii, he explained, his parents were both Japanese and he spoke Japanese fluently.

Tony didn't waste any time in introducing me to the manager of the health club, and it wasn't long before we had worked out an agreement by which the manager would rent me the space at the front of the club every morning and evening for karate classes. In return I would pay him a percentage of my students' fees. Three weeks later, when I opened for karate classes at the health club, I had Tony Hamada to thank for getting me started. Tony would remain a generous friend, helping me find sponsors and financial backing years later when I started organizing tournaments.

In August we held a Grand Opening at the health club, and Humberto Leon, Greg Vahenian, and Vernon Brown all came out from New York to help get things organized. We had a large sign painted and placed it in the window, and by opening night we had signed up ten students. A month later enrollment had jumped to thirty. With thirty students kiaiing in the front of the health club, some of the regular members started to complain that we were making too much noise and taking up too much space. But I couldn't very well ask my students to whisper their kiai, and the fact was we would need even more room than we had. I talked with the manager and he agreed to give us some extra space. Little by little, we kept expanding until we had taken up more than a third of the club's floor space.

Although the health club members gradually accepted us, and some of them even became students of mine, there were people on the outside who weren't as friendly and didn't hesitate to let us know we weren't welcome. One morning I arrived at the club to find the windows covered with black grease, and another time my car was vandalized right in front of the club. I don't know whether another karate school was unhappy about our style setting up in their neighborhood, but clearly someone in the area didn't like us invading their turf. Finally, one of them stepped forward and issued a formal challenge I could do something about.

That challenge came one day during one of my morning classes. A visitor entered the club and sat down on a bench near the door. He was tall and well built, and throughout the class studied the students and me very closely. It wasn't unusual for prospective students to watch a class before signing up, so I didn't think much about him. After class I went over and asked him if he were interested in training with us.

He said he was already training in tae kwon do and that he came because he wanted to spar with me. He was polite enough, but there was a chip on his shoulder and a tone of cockiness that rubbed me the wrong way. It didn't take long for my students to get wind of the challenge. Naturally they wanted to stick around to see how I handled it. Suddenly I remembered the curiosity of the students in the dojo in Matsuyama, where I had turned up unexpectedly to challenge the sensei (teacher). As a sensei I had never been challenged by an outsider, and I certainly had no intention of backing away from this one. Still, I had to be sure the stranger understood the seriousness of his challenge.

"If you mean that you want to just practice or play around, I'm not interested," I said. "But if you're challenging me, I'll do it."

He said he was serious, so I pointed to the dressing room. A moment later he came out dressed in a plain white gi and black belt. We squared off in the middle of the floor, and I waited to see what he could do. He snapped several kicks, and a few landed on my chest and shoulders. They were surprisingly fast but had very little power behind them. I waited until he had finished, and then I piled into him with a combination of kicks and punches. I pinned him against a cabinet and finished him with a roundhouse kick to the face. When he collapsed on the floor, the blood from his mouth spotted the front of his gi. My students were gaping at me in disbelief. They had been practicing karate with me for only a few months, but until that moment they hadn't seen it used in a serious confrontation.

The stranger dragged himself into the dressing room, and when he came back out in his street clothes he was gingerly testing his lip with his finger. The bleeding had stopped, and he tried to make a joke at his own expense—something conciliatory I can't recall. I do remember that his lack of pride made my stomach turn. I wasn't interested in being friendly, and it just wasn't in me to laugh away a challenge with a slap on the back. I had no patience for fools who played at fighting.

As for my students, I couldn't worry about how a little blood affected them. Kancho had taught me to face challenges decisively, and I knew no other way. Maybe students in America expected something else from their teachers. After all, this was the land of "fair play" and "good sportsmanship." But I couldn't change what I was. I couldn't "play" at fighting and I would never do karate only halfway. I could still picture the dojo in Matsuyama where the teacher had refused my challenge only a few years before. I remembered the empty building and the "For Rent" sign in the window. I might frighten students away from time to time, but if I ever ended up with an empty dojo, it wouldn't be because I had backed down from a challenge.

The 1977 All-Japan came and went that fall, but not without a few rough days and a lot of hard memories. Kancho called to tell me with the results, and I pretended not to care. Inside I ached with the rotten luck of having cut my thumb. I kept thinking about what I could have done that year if I had been healthy. And the stupidity of it—the pain, the days in the hospital—it all gnawed at me again for days on end, and I couldn't shake the bitterness.

I tried to keep busy so I wouldn't have time to feel sorry for myself. I trained even harder than usual, punishing myself. I did a lot of running outdoors, and when winter came I pushed myself out into the snow. The colder it was, the more I liked it.

My first winter in the West was one of the coldest on record, and the air burned against my lungs like dry ice. I developed a bad cough and finally had to run in a mask to help warm the air before it reached my lungs. In Japan, of course, there is nothing unusual about wearing a mask on the street when one has a cold, but in the United States they are very generous about sharing their germs. A mask on the streets of Denver was an oddity, and everyone kept telling me I looked like a surgeon.

The snow that first year was knee deep and stayed on the ground all winter long. Still, I was out each morning even during the coldest spell when the ice clogged my nostrils. One morning my eyelids stuck together. I was suddenly blind and thought there was something wrong with me, until I realized the moisture in my eyes had turned to ice and frozen my eyelids shut.

My thumb was healing, but still posed a problem. I had to wrap it each day for training, and in the cold the blood hardly seemed to flow through it at all. If I stayed outside too long, it felt as though it were made of glass—one knock and it would break into a hundred little pieces.

The summer of 1977 finally arrived, and I had completed a full year of teaching classes at the health club. But the last few months had been uncomfortably cramped, and there was no escaping it: I needed more space. The time had come for me to open a dojo of my own.

In July we moved out of the health club. I still hadn't located another dojo, so during August we held class outside, training in the same park where I had first set up my heavy bag the year before. Finally I located a vacant store on Pearl Street only a few blocks from the health club location. We opened in September, and again Humberto Leon came out to lend a hand. Right away I put him to work as "the bouncer."

Most dojos don't need a bouncer, but our new location was right next to a bar. The jukebox cranked up each night right at six o'clock just when our classes started, and the music would come pounding through the wall, drowning out all of my instructions to my students. I complained to the management next door, and they turned down the volume. I wished they could have done something about the flow of drunks that washed through our door each night. They'd stumble across the carpet and interrupt class with their drunken antics. That's when Leon "bounced" them out onto the sidewalk. Usually they went peaceably, but twice we had our front window kicked in by angry drunks who wanted to show us their own brand of martial arts.

When Leon wasn't sweeping drunks out onto the sidewalk, he was training with me. Each morning we began our workout by driving out to Lookout Mountain in the foothills overlooking the city, where we trudged up and down the steep hillsides. I had read about Olympic athletes who had boosted their performance in Mexico City by training at high altitudes. I was determined to do the same. Denver was a mile high, but I wanted to go even higher and harder. So we ran up the steep pastures, our ears popping, lungs burning. I even found a pair of heavy old boots that I wore to make the going rougher.

After returning to the dojo, Leon and I would work out with weights and bag-train. We kept to the same routine all year, and I continued sparring each day with my students for extra conditioning. It kept my reflexes sharp. I was hungry and ready, and after missing the All-Japan in 1977, I resolved to make 1978 my year. The thought of finally achieving my goal drove me out into the elements day in, day out, even on the coldest winter day when it seemed as if the earth would never warm again. The seasons passed in their slow cadence, and my body and will toughened like one of those gnarled pines clinging to a craggy mountainside, indifferent to extremes of heat and cold.

It was spring of 1978. The snow had disappeared. I was training in the park, and the sun burned hot again. My spirits were warm, and the disappointment of missing the 1977 tournament was a thing of the past. Nothing could bring me down now.

Then, one night, I was awakened by a phone call. It was my second-oldest sister, Tomiko, on the other end. The connection sounded fuzzy, but finally her voice came through, jagged and small as she struggled to hold back the tears.

"Father has died," she said.

The next morning, I caught a flight back to Japan. I had plenty of time to close my eyes and remember. . . .

I could still picture my father walking up the hillside with his ax and rope. I could see him picking out a stout, straight pine, chopping it down, and dragging the naked trunk down the mountain. On the grassy river bed in front of our house, he would strip the bark, and only after he had sawed it lengthwise would he take it to the sawmill at the hardware store. All of this my father did by hand, with care and attention. It was the only way, he claimed, to make straight smooth boards.

I realized on that flight home just how much of my father's sense of care and workmanship I had brought to karate. It had made me strive to master the most complex combinations with precision, and the example of his quiet determination had nourished me through the hardest challenges. Over the last five years I had seen my father only once each year, at the tournament in Tokyo. But even with an ocean between us, I had gotten into the habit of picturing him so often that I still felt he was just around the corner if I needed him. Those memories were so vivid, I think I even believed that somehow I would still see him when I got back to my village.

The reality didn't fully hit me until I got home. The weather had been hot, and my family told me they had to go ahead and perform the cremation. All that remained was the funeral and the burying of my father's ashes at our plot in the cemetery on the hill. I felt unprepared to say good-bye to my father. I had been away so long. If only I could have some of that time back . . . but it was too late now.

Over the next few days the dull ache of that loss sharpened into an unbearable pain that tore me apart inside. I had been off in America pursuing a dream, and what did I have to show for it? A few empty years, a severed thumb, my father gone. In my anguish, I was like a child throwing a tantrum. I was kicking over everything I had ever valued or worked for, spilling out their contents on the floor. I felt angry at the world for having robbed me of my father. I didn't let it show, but inside the bitterness ate at me, and I realized I was giving in to the defeat of self-pity. This was the last thing my father would have wanted. "Be strong. Try hard." Slowly I pulled myself together.

They told me that my father had gone up into the hills to cut timber for a house he was going to build. He didn't come home that night, and when my brothers went searching for him, they found him near a tree that he had cut down. Evidently, he had been stripping off the branches and had had a heart attack. Unable to move, he had lain there helplessly, loosening his belt to make himself more comfortable. Perhaps he had called out for help, but no one had heard.

It seemed like a very hard way to die. Everyone thinks of dying peacefully in bed, perhaps during sleep. But I don't think my father would have wanted that. He died the way he spent his life, alone in the woods at his work. And the nature of his death made me respect him more for the way he had lived his life. When his name is mentioned now, I still imagine him sawing the length of a log by hand with absolute attention and precision.

The trip home for my father's funeral made me realize how much he had given me. So many of the things I still enjoyed and cared for had been introduced to me by my father: the stories of Musashi that he read to me as a child, his love of drawing, his handiness with tools and brush and ink. He believed it was important to be able to do many things well . . . to apply one's skill and attention to any kind of task and perform it competently. All of this he gave to me.

After the funeral I stayed a few weeks in Japan, training at the dojo in Matsuyama. Finally, when I returned to the United States, I felt as though my father were closer to me than ever. I was still teaching and training every day, and I felt as if he were looking over my shoulder, making sure that I did my job right. . . .

Why is it that we never understand or appreciate those for whom we care so deeply until it's too late?

Seven months after my father's funeral, I was back in Tokyo for the 1978 All-Japan Open Karate Tournament. For the last ten years this had been the object of my every effort. Although first place had eluded me—for lack of skill, or stamina, or just bad luck—this year I was ready, and nothing could change that.

Ten years of spirit and striving had focused on this one event, and somehow, intuitively, before the tournament even started, I sensed that this would be my year. It is difficult now to describe just what that sensation was like, except to say that I felt I was in the hands of a larger force.

Over that last half year since my father's death, I had rededicated myself to karate. It sounds odd now to say that. I wonder how many times I have "rededicated" myself to my art. Yet, looking back now, I can see that there are levels to karate. The movement through those levels is punctuated by moments of clarity and absolute understanding, moments that energize the spirit and drive you deeper and deeper into that art. As you delve deeper, you discover more than technique, more than how to win tournaments. You are put in the hands of a larger, indefinable force that gradually sculpts your character to a purpose whose certainty feels nothing short of destiny. In Tokyo in 1978, I could feel the hand of destiny resting on my shoulder.

A few days before the start of the tournament, Kancho and I were waiting in a restaurant for our meal. He was attempting to describe a combination that he had been working out in his mind. Finally words failed him. "Stand up," he said. We pushed back our chairs and I was on my feet facing him in fighting stance. "Throw a right punch," he commanded.

How many times had I been with Kancho when he insisted on showing a technique in the middle of a crowded sidewalk, restaurant, or hotel lobby? I was used to the attention it drew, the sudden whispers. The room turned quiet with anticipation. I could sense the faces of other diners looking up at us with fleeting expressions of concern as I slowly threw the punch and Kancho answered with a quick combination, explaining his movements. Twice more he demonstrated the technique with a slight variation. The diners sensed that this was not a real fight. They were smiling at the realization, as though a joke had been played on them, and they went back to their meals, still glancing up every now and then as the waiters cut careful detours around us. "Let me see that again," Kancho said.

Knowing Kancho and his single-minded devotion to karate, I had come to expect these impromptu demonstrations anywhere, at any time. Kancho was like an artist who would pull out a sketch pad and pen any time an image struck his creative fancy. One morning, in our room at the Prince Akasaka Hotel, he and I pushed furniture out of the way, making space in the middle of the floor for *sabaki*—a form of controlled sparring practiced in the dojo. Many of the techniques he showed me in that session could not be used in tournament competition; they were meant for the street, for actual life-threatening situations, where no judges or referees would be standing by. "That was *real* karate," Kancho explained later as we got into the elevator. "*Jissen* karate." The other passengers stepped to the rear. "What if you were attacked in an elevator or in a narrow corridor?" Kancho asked with a knowing smile.

The few days I spent with Kancho before the tournament were packed with such lessons and fine tunings. Meanwhile, I continued to run each morning in the park, stretching and doing calisthenics in the hotel room.

My mother and brothers arrived the day before the tournament started. In my father's absence my family seemed quiet, perhaps full of sad memories. Annoying as it had been at times, I now missed my father's coaching. I would have given anything to have him back in the crowd or even traipsing after me into the locker room to deliver a post-fight lecture on what I should have done. Privately I resolved to fight this All-Japan for him.

Finally the tournament started, and I moved easily through the first few rounds. With each fight I seemed to grow stronger. After taking a decision in my first round, I won each successive fight with a knockout until I reached the semifinals.

In the semifinals I faced Mr. Makoto Nakamura, a two-hundred-pound fighter from Tokyo headquarters who had won every round by knocking out all of his opponents. Size meant nothing to me now. Although I was two years younger than Mr. Nakamura, I had been fighting for ten years, and I had far more fighting experience, especially against large fighters in the United States. For all I cared, Mr. Nakamura could have been a mountain; I wasn't going to let him stand in my way. The path I had traveled in karate was too long and too rough for me to think of losing this fight. I vowed to myself that if I lost to Mr. Nakamura, I would quit karate forever.

As confident as I felt, I still had to plan my strategy carefully. From watching Mr. Nakamura's previous fights, I knew he always attacked with a left straight punch and followed it with a right-left combination, slapping his opponent's left arm out of the way before finishing with a left roundhouse kick. The slap alone was very powerful and had doubled up most opponents, making them vulnerable to the roundhouse kick. I was going to make sure Mr. Nakamura never got the chance to use it on me.

At the opening drum Mr. Nakamura barreled at me with a straight left punch. I quickly jumped outside and countered.

After a decision in my first round match of the 1978 All-Japan,
I won each successive fight with a knockout
until I reached the semifinals.

*Early round action from the 1978 All-Japan Tournament.
This low roundhouse kick took down my opponent
and scored a half point.*

*This front kick took down Mr. Makoto Nakamura and scored
a half point in the semifinals of the 1978 All-Japan.*

Twice more he came at me the same way, and twice more I jumped outside and attacked his ribs and chest with solid punches and front kicks. Then, in the middle of the round, I caught him with a solid roundhouse kick to the jaw. Somehow he managed to stay on his feet, and I began to wonder if I would need an elephant gun to bring him down. I threw left front kicks to keep him at a distance, but he kept trying to catch my legs and throw me backward. He couldn't get me down, though, and with fifteen seconds left I sensed that he was getting impatient. He came at me with a right roundhouse kick. As soon as I saw it coming, I countered with a left front kick that reached his solar plexus just at the height of his kick. He fell backward and went down. I was awarded a half-point and won the fight.

In the final round I was to face Mr. Keiji Sanpei, whom I had defeated in the quarter finals in 1976. Stamina was no longer a problem for me. The closer I came to making my dream come true, the more energy I seemed to have; if I had to, I was ready to keep on fighting all night long. I was particularly looking forward to this final match, because I knew from past experience that Mr. Sanpei had a strong fighting spirit. Whatever the outcome, it would be a good finale.

Right from the beginning, I attacked Mr. Sanpei with front kicks and low kicks. Mr. Sanpei answered with a barrage of punches and low kicks. Neither one of us backed away, and the fighting stayed extremely close. We both were determined to win, and our spirit was so intense that it felt as if there were enough energy on that mat to light up a city.

The first round ended in a draw, and during the one-minute rest period the crowd worked itself into a frenzy. Ten thousand voices divided into two camps shouting our names back and forth—Sanpei. . . Sanpei. . . Ninomiya. . .

Ninomiya! Again I felt I could win. No matter how many over-times we might face, I knew I had the spirit and stamina. I felt as if the energy of the crowd were flowing directly into my body.

The overtime was again very close, and the two of us fought as though our lives depended on the outcome. Every ounce of our strength poured into each punch, as our bod-ies arched together over the mat. Dimly, I sensed the two of us locked together in a timeless attitude, like two warriors struggling on an ancient vase. The noise of the crowd was like the roar of a gigantic wave that lifted us both to a final heroic effort. Then the bean bag suddenly skidded across the mat, signaling the end of the match, and the final drum boomed.

I remember the sound of the crowd echoing under the high ceiling of the gymnasium as we pulled ourselves apart and took our positions on opposite sides of the circle. The audience suddenly hushed to an eerie silence, waiting for the decision. Then the judges raised their flags. The deci-sion was mine. The crowd roared again. I had finally won the All-Japan.

I bowed and immediately looked for Kancho. When he stepped up onto the corner of the platform, I ran over, shook his hands, and bowed. We didn't need to say a word. I could see the approval in his eyes. Through the din of applause and the glare of flashbulbs popping, I retreated to the center of the mat with the image of my teacher's face in my mind. I knew that Kancho was the happiest man in the whole gym-nasium, and I felt gratified finally to have been able to give him that satisfaction.

Vaguely, I heard the announcer calling the fighters up for the awards presentation. We lined up. My name was called, and a document was read. The trophy was presented, and I bowed. I tried to hold back the tears that filled my eyes. I had reached the top of the mountain and the view was humbling in its magnificence. I wished my father had been there to share it. I cannot describe the joy and sadness that overwhelmed me at that moment.

After the tournament, Kancho and I traveled around the country, visiting dojos in Osaka, Matsuyama, and Yawatahama. There was a party at each dojo and a great deal of fanfare, and I suddenly found that I wasn't quite prepared for all the attention now focused on me. In each dojo I was expected to give a speech to encourage the students, and I found myself not knowing what to say. Over the years my world had been an isolated one, limited to daily workouts in an empty dojo and the routine of teaching in the evenings. It was difficult for me to speak in front of a group of strangers, and this new responsibility posed a different kind of challenge. I had always admired Kancho's easy way of speaking and taking control of a group. I would rather have fought three Mr. Sanpei than stand up to talk in front of an audience. I tried to keep my message simple: I explained that my victory in the All-Japan was not accomplished without the help of many friends, especially Kancho. This was not just a rhetorical kindness on my part; it was fact. Without Kancho's wide range of techniques, I would have been a limited fighter. He showed me the importance of doing many things well, and only by mastering many different techniques could I keep larger opponents off balance. Against fighters like Mr. Nakamura and Mr. Sanpei, this was critical.

Always, at these parties, the students mobbed me afterward, asking for autographs. Strangers approached me on the street and asked for a signature. One man in Osaka even asked me to sign a picture of his newborn infant. He told me he never missed my fights, and named his baby Joko in my honor. It is an unusual name, and I felt proud and oddly touched to hear that someone—a total stranger—had passed it on.

I had heard that some champions found this exercise of signing autographs a tiresome chore. But to me there wasn't a question of liking it or not. I considered signing autographs a duty that came with the territory, so to speak. I never refused because I remembered how much I had once looked up to champions, and I knew what a difference it made to receive attention from someone I admired. I was happy to be able to give some of that back. If I could be a good example and help out a youngster, it was well worth the time it took to sign my name. I always added "*Doryoku*" ("Effort") because I wanted them to remember, even when things seemed difficult, to keep trying hard.

Our last stop on the tour was Yawatahama, where I received a victorious homecoming from family and friends. Mixed with the happiness of this occasion, however, was the sorrow of knowing my father would not be there to share in the celebration. It was going to take time to get used to that. I had brought along a small copy of my trophy, and I placed it in the butsudan, the shrine in my family's home, to let my father's spirit know that my victory was for him.

Finally I returned to Denver, where I was met at the airport by my students. We had a raucous celebration at the dojo, and for a few days my spirits were high. But then, gradually, reality descended once more. Although enrollment was healthy at the dojo, costs were rising. Rent, electricity, insurance: everything went up, and although the dojo broke even, money was short. I would have to find a way to bring in additional funds just to make ends meet. That winter I went to work as a construction worker.

The irony of my situation was painfully clear. Only a few weeks ago I had been honored with karate's highest award, but Denver was not Matsuyama or Tokyo. Outside of the dojo, I was hardly known in my adopted city, and there was no way to turn my title into a steady income. Sometimes during those cold winter days as I worked outdoors, I thought of how comfortable I could have been back in a warm dojo in Japan. Day after bone-chilling day, perched on a rooftop, hammering shingles, I tried to squeeze warmth from the hard western sunlight and draw it into my body. Sometimes I questioned my stubborn resolve: Why not just go home to Japan? Hadn't I climbed the mountain? Hadn't I reached the top? What else was there for me to prove?

Of course I already knew the answer to that. In the days following the All-Japan, as I traveled the country with Kancho, I had made my decision. I knew that the 1978 tournament would be my last. I wasn't leaving karate—only that protected world of tournament competition with its rules and referees. I had been concerned all my life with competition, with winning and losing. As a youngster it had been helpful to have concrete goals, but now that I had more experience it was time to move on, time to seek real karate—jissen karate. There was a deeper challenge for me that lay ahead, and that path was just beginning to unfold.

Ahead lay the inner challenge of bushido and frontiers to explore beyond the edge of the tournament mat. These rewards would be much greater than a gold-plated trophy, just as karate itself was much greater than any single tournament or fighter. I had reached the top; yet, as Senpai Kishi had warned, I could not stop climbing or the challenge of bushido would die. The challenge I faced in Denver that winter was just another beginning.

That March, as spring reluctantly returned to the Rockies, I spotted an ad in the paper that asked for a karate instructor to teach at what I first thought was a private school. The money was good, and I jumped at the chance of teaching karate part-time in addition to my regular classes at the dojo. I met with Mr. Sonny Emerson, the man who ran the school, and we hit it off right away. He hired me and provided everything I needed to get the program off on the right foot.

As it turned out, the school was a halfway house for kids who had been in trouble with the law and were making the transition from jail back into society. Some of the wards at Emerson house had been involved in burglaries or shootings. They were tough kids in their late teens, and many of them had the fully developed bodies of grown men. I was responsible not only for teaching karate, but for organizing a recreational program as well. That meant I was supposed to find ways to keep about a hundred very troubled Indians, Cubans, and Chicanos meaningfully occupied when they weren't busy with classes in reading and math.

They were violent kids, and the various groups were constantly at one another's throats. Mr. Emerson thought that a karate program might help some of them channel that energy more productively, but he warned me that it wouldn't be easy. In the past two years he had already gone through five instructors. I was number six, and from the very first day the kids were betting among themselves that I wouldn't last more than a month or two. The challenge only made me try harder.

I wasn't worried about how tough the kids were at Emerson House. I knew that underneath everyone was the same, with the same fears and the same need for acceptance. My job would be to build some of the confidence that had been missing in their lives.

The first thing I did was break up the groups. In karate class I paired off Cubans and Indians, Chicanos and Indians—any combination to break the kids out of their group mentality and force them to start seeing each other as individuals. At first they resisted learning the basics of karate instruction; they were more interested in showing how tough they were. As far as they were concerned, I was still an unknown quantity. I had come in and broken up their routine, upset their pecking order, and naturally the ringleaders didn't like it. They were waiting for a chance to challenge me directly and put me in my place.

I knew it would only be a matter of time, so I wasn't surprised when I arrived at work one afternoon and found everyone smiling like Cheshire cats. As I rounded up the students for class, a muscular, heavyset Indian who was built like a dump truck swaggered over and flung down the gauntlet.

"I've seen this karate stuff you're teaching," he said, poking his finger at me, "and I don't think much of it. What's more, I don't think you'd be much good without those kicks and punches. I used to be a wrestling champ, and I think I can take you down. What do you say?"

The others would have liked nothing more than to see the big Indian squash me like a bug, and it was clear from the way they were snickering that he had already boasted to them about how he was going to take me apart. I didn't hesitate.

"We'll do it in the gym," I said.

The others ran ahead, giggling and laying odds on how the big Indian would pin my ears back. They gathered around the boxing ring, clinging to the ropes, and waited. I didn't know wrestling rules, but I knew the unspoken rules of a challenge: I'd have to take the Indian down and keep him there.

We climbed into the ring and circled each other for a moment, as I waited for my opening. Finally he lunged at me with his big arms spread like an ape. I grabbed his neck, pulled down his head, then stepped in and threw him over my hip in an *uchimata* (judo throw). He fell to the mat like a sack of rice. I wrapped my legs around his neck in a *sankaku jime* (a judo choking technique), closing my right leg around his throat like a vise. He couldn't move, and he couldn't breathe. I held him until his face turned blue and he started gurgling. Then he passed out.

I pushed on his stomach to revive him, and a moment later he came to. He got to his feet and wobbled off into the corner without a word. There wasn't a sound. "Line up," I ordered.

After that the big Indian started training in karate every day. I noticed a big change in the others as well. They started paying more attention, and I no longer had to go looking for them before class. Instead I found them lined up and waiting for me in the gym when I arrived. It wasn't too much longer before I even started to get friendly with some of them. They began to think of me as an older brother. I took them out on field trips to the park, to pro-wrestling matches—anything to give them a sense of freedom and the responsibility that went along with it. My job didn't require me to play with them; I only had to supervise. But I always tried to participate even if it meant getting out on a basketball court with them so they could teach me to dribble or letting them show me how to shoot pool. Giving them a chance to teach me skills boosted their confidence and gave them a good feeling about themselves.

Many of those kids had never had an adult offer real friendship or warmth. Those who could return it were the lucky ones; they hadn't been hardened yet to the point of cold indifference, which is what drives some kids into serious trouble. Unfortunately, for some of them it was already too late.

One day I arrived at work and found everyone gathered in an upstairs corridor in front of one of the dorm rooms, peeking cautiously through the little window in the door. Inside, an eighteen-year-old Cuban had gone berserk. He had stolen an X-Acto knife from the office and had already slashed his wrists and ankles. The room was smeared with blood, and he had backed himself into the far corner, brandishing the razor-sharp blade at anyone who dared to step inside. I watched with frustration as the guards attempted to rush inside and subdue him, only to be driven out when he waved the blade in their faces. It was clear to me that if someone didn't get him out soon, he might bleed to death. I wasn't thrilled at the prospect of facing a blade in the hands of a crazy man, but there was no choice. I said I would give it a try, and the guards nodded eagerly.

I slipped through the door, and the Cuban bolted to the middle of the floor, waving the knife at me. His wild eyes kept darting from me to the door and back again. I had my jacket in my hand, and I waited until his eyes pulled to the door again; then I flung the jacket in his face, stepped in, and swept both his legs with a low kick. He went down and dropped the knife. I kicked it into the corner and held him until the guards came in. He kicked and spat and tried to bite me, but finally the guards tied his arms and legs, and rushed him off to the hospital.

The Cuban was transferred to a psychiatric ward, and we never saw him again. He was just another one of the lost souls, another tormented man-child who would never be touched and could never be saved. I saw a lot of young men like that at Emerson House, and I'll never forget the look of lonely desperation in their eyes.

Seeing so many of these kids without families, goals, or self-respect made me want to help. With some I failed, but it was important for me to have at least tried. That effort made my work at Emerson House more than a job. And karate, as I taught it, was more than a physical education requirement. The full contact against pads allowed the kids to release their aggression in a controlled way. They were learning practical techniques that could be used on the street, if necessary. Karate boosted their confidence, and promotion from belt to belt gave them a sense of accomplishment.

Karate gave structure and purpose to the lives of many of the kids at Emerson House. I developed friendships with some of them that lasted for years. Several continued to train with me at the dojo long after their release. Even today some of these men still visit me, and when I look at the pictures they bring of wives and small children, I feel warm inside for having made even a small difference in their lives.

Five

In 1980 Kancho left the Kyokushin organization and started his own style—Ashihara Karate. I left with Kancho and
became the United States director of Ashihara Karate. Over
the next eight years, Ashihara established itself as the
fastest-growing karate style in Japan. In the United States its
popularity continued to grow, but more slowly. Unlike
Japan, the United States does not embrace martial arts as an
integral part of its culture. Although attitudes have changed
recently, for many years Americans were suspicious of
karate. A number of movies in the late sixties and early sev-
enties sensationalized the martial arts and created precon-
ceptions that made it difficult to educate Americans in a
new, practical style they had never heard of before. Even so,
my dojo gradually increased in size and new schools started
to open in other cities. We moved into an even larger dojo in
east Denver and faced the challenge of reaching out to people of all ages and touching them with the spirit of real karate.

I suppose every student reaches a point in his training
when he decides it's time to leave his teacher and move on.
It is a point in the relationship between teacher and student
that is worked for and anticipated but not talked about very
much. There is an old budo belief that the teacher always

wants his student to surpass him. It is considered one of teaching's most profound rewards to watch a student move beyond his teacher, to develop his own understanding until his movement and discipline are a fully individualized expression of himself and no longer a mirror image of the teacher. Until that point, the relationship between teacher and student is one of respect and obedience. Too casual a relationship causes a loss of respect; too much control only burdens the student's spirit. Kancho always said there had to be freedom between a teacher and his student. He believed it was important to keep "a little play in the wheel."

After twenty years under Kancho's tutelage, I had given little thought to going off on my own. In an organization you follow orders from above. You structure your own school and its teachings after the pattern set by the leader. I had been comfortable with Kancho as a teacher. For practicality and effectiveness I considered his techniques unparalleled, and yet over the years I had developed strategies and ideas of my own that I was eager to implement. Kancho's generosity and support had always been unqualified, and our relationship had been close. As I said, I had never thought about going off on my own. Everything in my karate life I had done with Kancho in mind. After he formed his own style and I joined with him, I thought only of how to spread his brand of karate. I had done my best. Starting from nothing, with little money to advertise this new style, I brought one student at a time into Ashihara Karate, and gradually the name spread. But now I was finding a different path. I was thinking of new techniques. I wanted to develop a tournament format that would provide a true test of karate skills. I wanted to be able to teach more of the inner qualities of karate as well. All of these considerations were important to me.

Now I had a decision to make. I could go on trying to teach Kancho's style, or I could pull away from Kancho and teach my own brand of karate. It was time to go out on my own, to build my own style, to begin again. As for my students, I would leave the decision to them; they could stay in Ashihara Karate, or they could follow me. Either way I would understand perfectly. The transition would be gradual, but I was excited at the prospect of drawing on many of my of own ideas that I had put on the back burner for so long.

For some time I thought deeply about this move. It would be an enormous challenge to break away and start over on my own. And after all, Kancho had really been the only teacher I had ever had in karate. Finally I made up my mind, and once my decision was made I felt I was ready to spread my wings and fly. But first, before I told anyone else, I had to tell Kancho. I sat down and wrote him a letter:

Dear Kancho,

Each day in Colorado now, it is growing warmer. It is starting to feel like summertime. I hope that you, your wife and family are healthy.

The days go by very quickly. I have been your student for almost twenty years. Until now, I have always thought only of Ashihara Karate, and have tried to make it grow little by little. I have always done this because I believe this style is very special.

I remember the image of you twenty years ago, when you were training by yourself in the Yawatahama police dojo. And fifteen years ago, when I left for the United States for the very first time, we were standing on the dock at Matsuyama. I was about to get on the boat, and you told me I looked cold, so you took off your scarf and wrapped it around my neck. I have carried that picture of Kancho with me for fifteen years.

But now we have changed, and so has our way of thinking. Our hearts are in different places. I don't want to be a burden to you any longer. I don't want to have the feeling that we are always pulling in opposite directions. And now I want to face the challenge of building my own ideas about karate-do in the United States.

I would be honored if you would look at my leaving as a father might look upon a child who grows up and moves away from his parents into the world on his own. Thank you for teaching and loving me like a father for all these years. As of today, I am no longer a part of Ashihara Karate.

I wish you, your wife, and family good health and every happiness in the future.
Sincerely,
Joko Ninomiya
May 30, 1988

I wrote the letter over three times because I wanted it to say just exactly how I felt. It was important for me not only to show respect for a man who had given me so much; I also didn't want any bitterness to remain between us. I didn't want to argue. I didn't want to carry any grudges.

As I dropped the letter into the mailbox, I felt I was dropping twenty years into a deep pool. But there was no turning back now. There would be no changing my mind. Like the samurai who decides to fight and lay down his life in battle if need be, I was committed 100 percent. Of those twenty years under Kancho's guidance, I can say that I have no regrets. There will always be many good memories.

Once my decision was made I had to tell my students and send a letter to all of my branch instructors. I honestly didn't know what to expect. I was ready to start over from scratch. Whoever wanted to come with me was welcome; we would move on and learn together. But I also knew that I could end up standing alone. And if that were the case, I was ready to go back to the park and hang my heavy bag from a tree in order to get students.

I wasn't sure I would have any of the instructors with me, or even many of my students. Still, I was determined to continue. It is the nature of karate . . . to continue, to come full circle and begin anew. This was a new challenge, and as with any challenge one doesn't know how it will turn out until it is under way. I had been at this point before: coming to train in the United States, arriving in Denver, starting to train again after the disappointment of coming so close to winning the All-Japan. Now I was undertaking the biggest challenge of all, one that would mean larger responsibilities and no support from Kancho back in Japan.

Yes, I was worried, but it was a worry that fed my confidence and made me resolve to try even harder. One must have a mixture of worry and confidence. If not, everything is either too hard or too easy, and nothing that is achieved is worth having.

When the first calls started coming in from instructors around the country, I was nervous about what they'd say. But one by one they told me that the name wasn't important; it was the man who counted. They said they would stay with me wherever I went. "Your decision," they said "is ours."

All of them said this to me, each in a different way. Some wanted to know my reasons; they knew how close I had been with my teacher, and they were surprised. Some of them asked a lot of questions, and I explained my decision as clearly and honestly as I could. Others simply accepted my move without a word. One instructor in the Northeast called to say he was with me 100 percent. When I started to explain some of the reasons for my breaking with Kancho, he interrupted. "You don't need to tell me anything. I don't need a reason to follow. You are my teacher and that is good enough."

A few days later I called a meeting in my own dojo to tell my students. After training we all sat down in a circle, and I told them my decision, explaining the reasons. When I finished, the room went quiet for a moment. Suddenly everyone started clapping.

Over the previous few days I had been thinking about a name for my new style. I didn't intend to use my own name, because I wanted to create a style that would be open to everyone and not belong just to one person. I also wanted a name that would reflect both my techniques and philosophy. This was very important because karate is much more than a series of movements or techniques. The inner dimension of a fighter, what he does with his mind and heart, is just as important as what he does with his fists and feet. Thinking about all of these things, I finally came up with the name *Enshin Kai.*

In Japanese *Enshin* means "heart of the circle." *Kai* means "group." I chose Enshin Kai because I wanted to give the sense of people coming together in a circle as a group or family. The "heart" character was especially important, because I wanted my students to meet one another in the dojo not as adversaries but more as family members ready to help one another. The circle also represented the circular movements that take a defender around the thrust of an attack and enable him to counter from his opponent's blind side. But there was also another meaning of the circle *En* in Enshin; the En character in Japanese also suggests an incomplete circle. Finally, I wanted to suggest that karate is a journey whose goal is never reached: a process and not an end that is most important. Enshin Kai captured these inner and outer qualities of what karate had come to mean for me over the last twenty years.

I had also given much thought to my new logo. I didn't want simply to use a series of cleverly stylized letters or an image of two fighters locked in combat. I wanted the design also to reflect a deeper meaning and express my philosophy of karate. So I chose a circle with a fist in the center, a familiar enough symbol that would stand for the power and spirit of karate. But then in the wide circle surrounding the fist I wanted to show a ring of shading moving gradually from white to black. This had several meanings. First, it represented the circular progress of training: moving from white to black belt and then starting over again. This is a familiar notion among martial artists. Attaining a black belt means that one is starting over and moving deeper into the discipline. That is why first degree is called *shodan*; literally it means "beginning" black belt. But the gradual movement from white to black and back to white again also symbolized the newness of mind that a student should have every time he steps onto the dojo floor. It means that even after white belt, brown belt, and black belt, the student should approach his karate with freshness and spontaneity. It means he should clear his mind and make it new, as if it were his first time—*shoshin*.

At the dojo meeting that night after training, I told my students the new name. I showed them the new logo and explained the significance of both. They were all very excited, and afterward they came up one by one and congratulated me. Their overwhelming support made me feel very strong inside.

A teacher is always gratified to see his students perform well and improve themselves step by step; that is the usual reward. But the support I felt from my students and instructors, their devotion and encouragement that night, made me feel the rightness of what I was doing. Their support and love were unconditional—just as it is in a family. And together, like a family, we have continued to grow.

When I was still in high school, training in karate in Yawatahama, my teacher built a new dojo. Mas Oyama came for the grand opening, and told us how he had dedicated himself to his training when he was young. He described how he had set a goal of doing one hundred thumb push-ups, and after that was able to bend coins in his fingers, and even knock out a bull with his fist. Mas Oyama told us that not only would karate make our bodies strong, but it would make our minds strong and give us the perseverance to make our dreams come true. He knew that karate had enormous power to change one's whole way of being, because he had seen it in his own life.

Mas Oyama had a deep, strong voice that filled the room and inspired me with its power and conviction. Then he talked about his top students spreading Kyokushin karate from Japan to other countries around the world. At the time, only five or six of his top students had gone to other countries to set up new schools. One of those instructors was located in Brazil. "Brazil is so large," Mas Oyama explained, "that he has to fly from one dojo to another. The world is a big place, but if your thinking is small your accomplishments will stay small too. You need to have large dreams and ambition if you want to grow."

As a farm boy in little Yawatahama, I was captivated; the idea of flying from one dojo to another seemed like a fairy tale, yet that story planted a seed. It showed me the power of dreams and helped me to focus my training. I didn't set out to grow a style of karate that would become bigger and bigger; I was only interested in being the best karateka I could be. After I left tournament competition I turned my attention to becoming the best teacher I could be, and fifteen years later I too was flying to visit various Enshin dojos around the world. I didn't plan it that way; it was as if I had awakened from a dream. But even today, with many schools around the world, the most important thing for me is the day-to-day training. Whether you have one school or one hundred, if you don't continue to train, you lose the spirit of what you are doing. I promised myself that I would never become so busy with the organizational duties of a large style that I would not have time to train. This must come first.

In 1995, twenty-five years after I trained on Kawanohama Beach and received the gift of eggs that nourished by body and spirit, I returned to my middle school in my hometown to give a speech. I had become somewhat well known for my career in tournament karate fighting and then going to the United States to bring authentic fighting karate to that country. Whenever I returned to visit Yawatahama, I was asked to give a speech, but I had always been too self-conscious about speaking in public. Over the years I came to understand my responsibility as a teacher and how important it was for me to share my experiences with younger people, so they would learn how to challenge themselves.

In my speech to the middle school I told them about my summer training on Kawanohama Beach, when the mysterious farm wife left eggs for me in a basket. I told how I realized that even when we are struggling and trying our hardest and things seem most difficult, we are never alone. This is the lesson I learned from the mysterious farm wife who left me the eggs.

I had always wanted to thank this woman in person but never found a way to do so. On the day I returned to my middle school and gave my speech, there were several television cameras and reporters covering my address. That night on the news, they did a story about my speech. Little did I know that in a neighboring town a family would be watching the TV news as they ate dinner with their grandmother. When they saw the report about the farm wife from their town and her gift of eggs 25 years before, the mother wondered out loud, "Who do you think that could be?" The old woman spoke up and said, "Why I think that was me."

It wasn't until I had returned to Denver that I received a call from my brother, who told me that the farm wife I talked about in my speech had called his home to say she had seen the TV story about my middle school speech. A year later I was back in Japan in my hometown and determined more than ever to meet the mysterious egg lady. This time my middle school had organized a special reunion for me and the farm wife. Again the TV cameras were rolling as we each were positioned behind a special curtain that separated us on the stage in front of several hundred students and teachers. When the curtain was raised, I saw standing in front of me a small elderly lady dressed in a gray suit—Mrs. Takawo Abe. She had tears in her eyes. We shook hands.

"I'm so happy to see you," I said. "After all these years, I still remember your special gift for me on that beach. I'm so happy to be able to thank you in person."

Twenty-four years after the daily gift of eggs mysteriously arrived at my training site at Kawanohama Beach, I met my benefactor—Mrs. Takawo Abe.

She then made a short speech to the students. "I'm now 90-years old," she said, "and I just wanted to see how the boy turned out whom I gave those eggs to. I was worried this whole year, since I saw him tell his story on TV, that I might not be able to be here today. I could have lost my memory, or fallen down and have to use a cane and not be able to come at all." She told how I was different than most of the young boys who had come to the beach to play, and how she wondered why I pushed myself so hard during my training. She said she felt pity for the way I drove myself to exhaustion. As she spoke, I remembered that summer and how I thought of myself like a small fish that had kept close to the shore, but was now trying to make itself strong enough to swim in the big ocean. I was determined to succeed or to die trying.

Twenty-five years later, what affected me most about Mrs. Abe's speech was when she told the students, "After watching that young man training on the beach, I was always waiting for a hero like him to emerge from my town. To be successful in your own lives, you need this same ambition, effort, and patience."

It wasn't until later that I learned that Mrs. Abe had embodied these same qualities in her own life. Seventy years ago, when she was eighteen-years old—at a time when young women from small towns in Japan never went off to their fulfill dreams in the big city—young Mrs. Abe traveled by herself to Tokyo to become a teacher. She didn't have the money for books or classes, so she decided she would become a gym teacher instead. After finishing her education, she returned to her town to educate its young people and share her values.

After the reunion at my middle school, Mrs. Abe invited me back to her town near where I had trained on the beach. The beach had changed somewhat in 25 years. There was a new sea wall, a new park, and other little changes. She pointed out where the bamboo huts had once stood, next to which I had pitched my tent. It seemed like only yesterday. Mrs. Abe made a point of telling me how much she appreciated my effort to meet with her and say thanks, especially now as younger people seemed to forget the little courtesies that can be so important. She said that leaving the eggs for me was a small thing. She didn't want to interrupt my training, and she didn't want to make a big production now about my thanking her for that gesture. But she admitted that all of the attention around our reunion had brought a great deal of excitement back into her life. Since then we have kept in touch, writing back and forth every few months.

My story would not be complete without telling about a very important person in my life. When we are young, we think we can do everything by ourselves. Over time we learn that no person is an island; we all need support and understanding. I have been very fortunate to find this in my wife, Sae.

Sae comes from my hometown. Although we didn't know each other growing up, once we met we discovered that we had much in common. Sae is a very positive person, and even when things seem toughest she knows how to keep her head up and encourage me. She always finds a way to lift my spirits. I know where some of these qualities came from; our decision to marry and live in the United States was not one that many Japanese parents would embrace for their only daughter. Many would want to keep their daughter safe and secure, close to home. But Sae's parents were different; they were truly happy from the bottom of their hearts, and even encouraged Sae to create a new life for herself and her husband in the United States. Sae's positive spirit is a quality that I have seen time and again, and it has lifted me often.

Today Sae is at home in her new country. As a former schoolteacher, she has been an important influence in shaping not only our immediate family, but the larger family of Enshin students and *uchideshi* (boarding students) at the *honbu* (headquarters). Like everyone else, I have learned much from her insightful advice and understanding.

Six

My "journey" goes on, but my account of that journey would not be complete without sharing some reflections of this unique way.

This last section is a meditation—random thoughts on many aspects of karate from kiai to tournaments. It does not attempt to capture everything or even what is best about the "empty-handed" way. It simply describes, according to my experience, what karate is.

An Old Way in a New Land

I carry on a tradition of karate that was handed down to me by my teacher. I have chosen to do this in America because I am convinced that karate offers a tradition from which Americans can strongly benefit. Deep down, it is something I believe the American spirit wants and needs very much.

It is important to use the Japanese expressions, the traditional gestures—bowing, saying "osu." Each one of these parts reflects the whole spirit of karate. These signs of respect are important, not for my own self-esteem, nor to remind me of my native country, but to reaffirm the special quality of concentration and purity of effort that belong in the dojo. It is the only way to learn.

I have been in this country for 26 years and I have observed how independent Americans are in their thinking; they believe firmly in their individuality. But there are two sides to every coin, and sometimes that individuality can be taken to extremes.

For example, there is one American custom that I have never been able to understand: If you are sitting in a restaurant and need help from a waitperson, you may ask only the one who is waiting on your table. If you should ask any one of the others, they will reply, "I'm sorry, that is not my table." In Japan, if you ask for help in a restaurant, anyone will jump to assist you. Why? Because in Japan everyone assumes responsibility for the restaurant and its customers' well-being. Responsibility is shared; it is not divided up into individual domains.

Similarly, each morning on a typical Japanese business street, you will find the merchants busily sweeping the sidewalk. They do not clean only the area in front of their respective shops, but move along the whole block and share in the clean-up for the entire area. The Japanese are group-minded and assume responsibility together. Americans are not selfish by nature, but they are not encouraged to help one another.

I was reminded of this difference between our cultures years ago by my own son Koichi. He was then five years old, an age at which he was learning in preschool to clean up after himself—sometimes the earliest lessons are the most important. When he spilled something, he was told not to wait for someone to clean it up for him, but had been instructed that it was "his" mess, and he must take care of it. One day, after I spilled something, Koichi quickly passed on the lesson; he pointed out the responsibility for cleaning up as he had learned it in school: "Daddy, that is *your* mess, and *you* should clean it up." If our responsibility truly extended no further than the tips of our fingers and toes, that would be fine. But we live in a society with others, and that means sharing the burden.

I have always tried to instill the feeling that the dojo doesn't belong to me alone. It belongs to all of my students, and we all share in the responsibility for taking care of it. I try to help my students discover that taking care of the floor or cleaning windows is, in a way, like grooming themselves. It is a way of purifying not only their bodies, but their hearts and minds.

Lower belts do not understand at first that a dojo can be a special place. They only see it as a kind of gymnasium, a workout space. They say, "Oh, it will only get dirty again. Why bother?" However, the point is to confer a specialness upon the dojo, not merely to keep it clean. The dojo is, after all, a space in which you perform a series of disciplined movements with great attention and care. You perform these movements not only to be able to defend yourself, but also in order to know yourself.

The attitude you bring into the dojo is very much a reflection of the way you view yourself. So in one sense, if you clean the dojo, you are cleaning yourself.

If you take that sense of care and attention to yourself and apply it to the dojo, it uplifts your environment. It is a way of reinforcing on the outside what you are hoping to achieve on the inside. And as that environment gives back the feeling of care, so the sense of attention and concentration is heightened within.

It takes time to become aware of the importance of this effort, and I don't tell my students they must have this feeling. They learn it from watching the upper belts and the way they care for the dojo. So much of what is learned in the dojo is acquired by following examples. Whether it is a straight back kick or the idea of shared responsibility, both come from the same place.

If your intention is strong, and you really want to help someone, you should go ahead and do it. This is the way I learned in Japan. If my teacher was sweeping, I would go over and ask if I could sweep for him. He might have said, "I'm okay," but I would still gently take the broom from his hands and sweep, because only doing so showed that I really meant to help. Words are never as strong as actions.

In this country, however, if a lower belt sees you sweeping, he rarely thinks to ask if he can help. He will stand there for a half hour, watching you sweep the floor, wondering to himself, "Gee, I wonder why my teacher is cleaning up our dojo," or "Maybe somebody else should do that for him." If it should occur to the lower belt to ask if he can help, and you say, "I'm okay," his initiative is still usually weak; he will simply take you at your word, shrug, and back away. If you're lucky, and he's extraordinarily motivated, he might ask, "Are you sure you don't want me to do that?" Since helping out is not natural to these lower belts, it takes a while for them to catch on. The point is, if you are intent on helping, it is not enough simply to think about it; you must carry it through.

In every aspect of life it is a good habit to follow up your thoughts with immediate action. Otherwise, your life is filled with good intentions that never become realized. In karate, as in life, thinking and doing should be one and the same. One who thinks too long before acting shows a beginner's mind.

This is not simply a matter of respect but applies to a fighting situation as well, in which spontaneity is critical. In fighting, if you see an opening, take advantage by immediately attacking. To react spontaneously without thinking— or "asking permission" or worrying too much about consequences—is to act with the immediacy of shoshin. Should a threat arise on the street, mind and body will respond as one. You see a piece of paper, you pick it up; you see a weed, you pull it; you extend an offer to help someone sweep, you follow up and take the broom from his hand. If you say you are going to do something, you must carry through and finish it directly. Lower belts learn this slowly through the example of their senpai.

Aiming Too High

The reason most students quit training after a month or two is laziness; they are not willing to commit to the challenge of hard work and discipline. Karate is a departure from most people's routines. It should make reasonable demands on them and not defeat them, but even so it often proves too much for some.

Those who stay with their training only a few months quit for different reasons. Often they have set their goals too high. They want too much too quickly. Karate is a slow process; it cannot be learned overnight. Students who expect too much of themselves have a very high opinion of their own abilities. That is why a little humility carries a student far. If he remains open to the training and does not pass judgment on every kick or block, he will last longer and have a deeper understanding of his karate. "Over time, even dripping water will wear a hole through the hardest stone."

Commitment

Sometimes if a student is not developing quickly enough for his own taste, he will blame the style and seek out another. If he cannot execute a perfect roundhouse kick in a few months, he will feel there must be something wrong with the style or the teacher. He will blame everything but his own effort. Students who jump to another style, or attempt to learn several martial arts at once, believe they have an advantage because they are learning many different special techniques. True, they may learn a few tricks, but their understanding usually remains shallow because the movements are not trained deeply into their reflexes. This takes time. Training in one style over several years is like following a river that is slow and deep and strong. Training in several styles at once is like exploring every tributary you come to. They may lead nowhere or dry up altogether in hot weather. This way leads only to uncertainty.

There is nothing wrong with learning from other styles. But be as strong as you can in one style first, then you have a firm base on which to build.

There was once a student visiting from another country. He was a very devout Muslim who said he wanted to learn everything he could about our style. He said he was dedicated to improving his technique and making it as good as he could.

After a month he stopped showing up regularly at the dojo. I learned that he had been training at several other dojos in town in different styles. When I asked him about this, he admitted that he had been training with other teachers who were friends in other styles but that he only wanted to learn some of their more useful techniques.

"You say you're a very devout Muslim," I said. "You don't eat pork. You say you don't even eat food that is prepared in the fat from pork. Do you play with your diet the way you play with your karate? Are you going to experiment with other religions, just because you're curious?" I asked. "Are you going to try Buddhism one day and Christianity the next? I know karate is not religion," I explained. "But if you are serious about learning anything, you can only learn one thing at a time. You can't learn karate one day and kung fu the next."

If a student is unhappy with his karate and finds another he likes, he should quit altogether instead of trying to do two at once. He should find the one he likes and give himself to it 100 percent. This will take not weeks or months, but years.

Some students are attached to the *idea* of karate. They try to learn and read everything they can about new techniques, or they are fascinated by the spiritual dimension, but they practice very little in the dojo. Karate is a path that you follow not with the mind alone, but the body as well. They both must be in the same place at the same time. This is usually the dojo.

Moving Zen

Kumite tells everything there is to know about a fighter and his spirit. In kumite there is no time for thinking, only action. Every facet of training in the dojo prepares us for this moment—to react as immediately as shade answers sunlight.

Hundreds of years ago, when the code of bushido began, the stakes were much higher than they are today. A flicker of hesitation, a split-second failure of nerve or concentration, could mean a severed limb or death. Against the sword there was no time to think. Technique had to be practiced until its movements had been trained deep down, beneath the mind, into the instincts and reflexes. Only spirit could animate the body's instantaneous response to the moment.

The samurai stressed the importance of putting aside the mind and the incessant chattering of the self by saying, "*Bushido shinukoto to mitsuketari*" ("The essence of bushido is to find how to die"). Today we place a much greater value on human life, and a fighter isn't expected to actually lay down his life. Today, "finding how to die" has a more philosophical significance. It means that we approach each moment of life with the same urgency and clarity that we would bring to a confrontation with death.

In karate-do, "finding how to die" means letting go of the self and its attachments to failure or success, to thought and emotion. It asks the karateka to empty his hands so he can fully grasp the moment.

By fate or circumstance, I was brought to the spirit of budo even long before I knew its name or had started training in the martial arts. As a boy I innocently marveled at the natural movements of the *tombi* (small birds of prey—kites) riding the soft currents of warm air lifting against the hillside orchards above my village. I sensed it in my father's concern and care for a carpentry job well done. I appreciated it in Kancho's effortless precision the first morning I met him in the Yawatahama police dojo. In New York I saw it again in Senpai Kishi's devotion to a simple way of life. Through karate I have found a similar expression of spirit within myself, and I continue to reach for that clarity of purpose and action in every moment. These are the conditions of budo and my life.

Shoshin

Shoshin means the freshness of inspiration that begins every action. To maintain shoshin, we should try to make our effort new by capturing the spirit of original inspiration and commitment that gave birth to that action. Over time, habit can set in and we can lose that original spirit. The first time your teacher tells you to break a board you may feel doubt or uncertainty. But once you resolve to do it, you think of nothing else except the center of the board. As a result, you focus your energy entirely on the break. The next time you may think, "No sweat, I've done this before," only to find that you could not execute the break because you were not focused. When you undertake anything, remember the challenge of having done it for the first time. The focus and concentration of energy that empowered you the very first time is called shoshin.

Karate is more than just a force, more than a method of self-defense. It is a way of living by giving full attention to the moment, no matter what the activity. Surveyor, mechanic, executive, or cook—the position makes no difference; a job performed in the spirit of karate-do is done with a selfless awareness of the moment itself. Its spirit is very much like meditation. It is only fitting that karate is often called "moving zen."

Kiai

When a student comes to the dojo and begins to train, the first thing I teach him is a loud shout from deep down in the belly. No matter how self-conscious or uncomfortable he may feel at first, I insist on a loud kiai, because it helps unlock the rhythm of the moment and brings the mind and body into the present.

I know it will take years before a student masters the techniques and form of our style, but the kiai is a must. It allows the beginner to get in touch with his spirit. And without spirit, there is only a body ready to be shaped by the thoughts already sitting inside its head. Kiai is the spark that ignites the spirit, burns away thought, and takes us into the rhythm of the moment.

I sometimes tell my children's class to think back to when they cried very hard to let their sadness out. I tell them to shout the same way when they do karate, so they can let out their power and energy. When you are tired or depressed, or distracted by the events of the day, the kiai will summon the spirit that can focus energy in the *seka tanden* (the lower

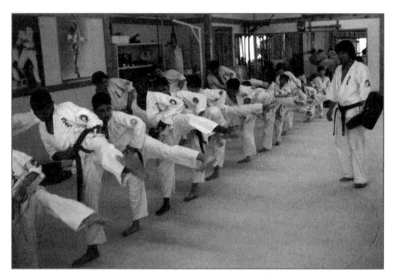

Children's class at the honbu, 1998.

abdominal area, housing the body's center of gravity, located between the navel and tailbone) and increase your strength. Instantly it will bring you back into the present and burn away the distractions that cling to the mind. Many times in the late rounds of a tournament, a loud kiai raised my spirits and gave me the strength to fight on. It was a way of telling myself, "*Yoshi-koi!*" (Come on, I'm ready for anything!")

The kiai is not just for the dojo or tournament mat alone. It can help you rise to any occasion. I once had an *uchi-deshi* who had a hard time getting out of bed in the morning for bag training. Inevitably, on my way to the dojo first thing in the morning, I would hear a low kiai as he pushed himself off the mattress and onto his feet.

A Little More Each Day

Training is a process of "self-creation." A teacher cannot create a fighter—he can only show the way. A student must take body, mind, spirit, and the given techniques, and from

Many times in the late rounds of a tournament, a loud kiai raised my spirits and gave me the strength to fight on.

these materials mold himself into a fighter. The best way to get anyone to change is a little at a time. In the dojo this may mean one extra push-up or an extra frog-jump, or stretching a little farther. It may mean making one's form on the last combination every bit as precise as it was for the first. Don't overwhelm or defeat yourself by making demands you can't meet. Make training a steady, manageable challenge, so that each day you do a little bit more. Never stop without having put forth that extra effort. "*Kyo wa kinouno jibun ni katsu,*" say the Japanese. "Try today to surpass the person you were yesterday."

When you are tired, and your muscles are burning, and you feel you can't go on, that last punch or kick is the one that will make you stronger. The fighter who bag-trains for three minutes and no more will only be able to fight for three minutes. But what if he has to fight for four minutes? What if he has to face a challenge on the street? Will he be able to reach down for anything extra if he's never given it before? During training, look upon that last stretch, that last punch or kick, like a friend, and he will stand by you when the going is toughest of all.

Training is an attitude—a way of thinking about effort and challenge, so that it becomes not only acceptable but something to be desired. In turn, training makes the tasks we face in everyday life that much easier.

Even with an injury, there is always something to do. If your leg is sore, work on punches. If your hand is injured, concentrate on kicks or kata. There is always something to be done to improve technique or strength. Regular training brings regular results, and once a student sees that for himself, training becomes a comfortable habit.

"-ing Karate"

Little by little, through sweat and effort, and by confronting his own worst fears, the student discovers "how to die," and he realizes that it is perhaps not such a terrible thing.

It is a simple problem; the student is asked to remember a sequence or combination, but he is told not to think about it. Thought will only interfere with that frictionless flow of movement. It will take time, practice, and a sense of surrender to reach down below the level of the mind to an understanding that is rooted in the muscles and nerves. Only after exhaustion, pain, and even boredom, can the body begin to perform what the mind cannot.

The movements of karate should be spontaneous, a concept sometimes called "-ing karate" because we intend it to take place totally in the present. Each movement and technique should flow like water in a mountain river, swirling and streaming on its course without a hitch or hesitation. If a fighter lets his thoughts interfere—thinking, I punched, then I kicked, what next?—his movements become labored. Instead of flowing together like a mountain stream, they break up into separate, jagged chunks of ice.

There is no secret to mastering "-ing karate." Training these movements deep into the body is a four-stage process. First is the job of memorizing the form—the sequences and combinations. The form is repeated as fluidly as possible without power or speed. When the student is comfortable with this, he adds speed, and then gradually increases power at the impact points. Finally, the ingredient that makes all of these elements come together is the dynamic force of spirit. So we have the four main components of Enshin karate—form, speed, power, and spirit. In every step of training we should be aware of these elements.

Even the black belt who encounters a new technique should be prepared to start by examining it one step at a time. This is the method for learning any form of karate and mastering a smooth, effortless execution. The degree of smoothness and speed is the difference between a blue belt and a black belt.

Sanding the Rough Spots

When students asks which part of training is most important, I tell them to look at their form, speed, power, and spirit and to ask themselves honestly, what is their weakness? This is most important. Keep up your strengths but work on your weaknesses.

Students who want to forget their weaknesses and concentrate only on their strongest techniques quickly become one-dimensional fighters—their tactics are inflexible. They don't last long in kumite because they can't adapt well to changing conditions or styles. A balanced fighter is the most effective because he is the most adaptable.

Never be satisfied. Work on your weaknesses. Concentrate on a technique or combination: Slow it down, take it apart step by step, and look for your flaws. Feel for the rough spots where balance is uncertain or the muscles unnecessarily tight. When you find that rough spot, sand it smooth by repeating it over and over until it feels right.

Stamina or Technique?

In the All-Japan competition, where I had to fight six matches in two days, I would have said that stamina was more important. But in an encounter on the street that lasts only seconds, technique is probably more important. Especially against a larger opponent, effective technique can make up for considerable size disadvantage. Ideally, however, one should be prepared for any kind of fighting situation, which means that stamina and technique are equally important. After all, what good is the best technique in the world if you don't have the stamina to execute it beyond the first minute or two of kumite?

Jissen

From my teacher I developed a system of karate that delivers great power from a practical combination of many small movements. This is Enshin's special quality of jissen. In one sense, jissen is the efficiency that draws the greatest power from the most compact of movements. In another sense, it is the economy of thought and action that arises spontaneously in a fighting situation. Jissen is the word that best describes Enshin karate, because it is based on real fighting. Enshin is in essence "jissen karate."

Sabaki

Sabaki is the heart of Enshin Karate. It is the transitional movement that occurs when a defender blocks and moves out of the line of attack into a position from which he can freely and most effectively control his opponent.

There once was an old sword master who was ready to retire. He had to choose between his two top students to see which one would take over leadership of his dojo. One day, the master and his top two students were walking down a road. The master stopped for a drink of water and sent his two students ahead. As he watched, the two students approached a slow-moving horse from the rear. Wary of the horse, Student 1 moved to the horse's side and continued past at a leisurely pace. However, Student 2 stayed behind the horse; when the horse suddenly bucked and kicked backward, Student 2 drew his sword in a flash and cut off the horse's leg before its hoof could even touch him. The villagers who had seen this astonishing feat crowded around the swordsman and applauded his lightning reflexes. The sword master approached the two students and announced, "Now my decision is clear. I choose Student 1." "But, master," exclaimed the villagers, "Student 2 has just shown remarkable speed and technique, which probably no one could match!" "Perhaps so," said the sword master, "but Student 1 sensed the danger before it showed itself, and he positioned himself to avoid the attack altogether. Often it's better to exercise judgment instead of reflexes."

The old way of countering an attack was to use any block and see if you could punch or kick your opponent before you got hit again. This was straight-in fighting, where the important thing was to hit first, and the result was more important than the process. This strategy was fine if you were quick or powerful. But it still wasn't very smart because you would always take punishment; your body was always in range directly in front of your opponent.

Use your head as well as your body. Ask any general what he believes is the single most important element in warfare, and he will tell you, "Positioning." In Enshin karate you think like a general but react like a cat. If an attack comes, first move out of the way. Move to a position from which you can see, and counter immediately. This position is always to your opponent's backside. He can't reach across his body to strike you, and he can't see you with both eyes to tell where your attack is coming from. You are in the best tactical position from which to counter. This is sabaki.

Let's think of it another way. If a car is rolling toward you, are you going to stand there and try to stop it? Of course not. Are you going to turn and start running away from it? Let's hope not. If you're thinking, you will probably move to one side or the other and then try to do something about the situation. You needn't move far, just enough to avoid impact.

The same is true in karate. You needn't move far to avoid a kick or punch, just enough to avoid the full impact. Then you can counter before your opponent recovers enough to continue his attack.

If the attack doesn't have much force, you can step to the outside of his attack and push him away with your blocking hand. His shoulders will rotate away from you, exposing his blind spot. If, on the other hand, his attack is quite strong— say, your opponent is lunging at you or he is too big to turn—then you must move to his backside. This is the essence of sabaki. It means moving out of the way of an attack into a position from which you can counter most strongly—your opponent's blind spot. It is a simple idea and very practical.

How can anyone fight intelligently without first considering his position? Let's face it, we are not always lucky enough to choose our opponents. If we were and could always face smaller fighters, we could hold our position and overpower them. But life is not always so kind, and odds are you will run up against someone bigger than you. When you're out-muscled, you have to use your head. You must create a strong position from which to keep your opponent off balance.

Position is critical, yet many fighters give no thought to this vital principle. They attack or counterattack straight in, but their techniques are not very effective because they are not combined with good positioning. They are simply not practical.

For example, I still see many karateka blocking a right front kick with a *gedan barai* (lower parry) or a left straight punch with a left *soto uke* (outside block). But these blocks still leave the defender open to an attack from the back hand. Unless the block is combined with positioning—the sabaki alternative—the defender stays at best only equal with his attacker, instead of moving into a position of tactical advantage.

Positioning means not only moving out of the way of an attack, but also being aware of distance and using the timing appropriate for each distance—short, middle, and long. Distance is not a function of where you start in relation to your opponent when you square off to fight; it is determined by where you find yourself at the end of his attack when you are ready to counter. You should always attempt to decide the distance best suited for countering your opponent, and then move accordingly.

There is not room enough here to go into much more detail on these matters. (For more on strategy and technique, see my book *The Sabaki Method*.) The important point—whether you follow sabaki or not—is to stay open to new techniques. Be ready to learn from anyone; otherwise, you stay a prisoner of your own ignorance.

Stay Open to New Ideas

I've always thought it important to keep myself open to new ideas. For this reason I consider myself equal with my white belts; it allows me to learn from them.

Once, not too many years ago, I was teaching *mawashi uke* (circle block). Mawashi uke consists of both hands circling simultaneously in a vertical plane in front of the body. The knife edge of one hand circles in an upward direction (palm out) as the knife edge of the other hand circles downward (palm in). Mawashi uke is practiced during basics as a formal technique used more for coordination and rhythm than for an actual fighting application, and for some reason, we always practiced mawashi uke with the upward blocking hand on the inside. However, on this particular day, I noticed that one of my white belts always did his mawashi uke with the blocking hand outside his front hand. Although I corrected him several times, he continued to do the block his own way. As I thought about it, I began to realize that his way was, after all, smoother and more natural.

In Japan with my teacher a few months later, we were preparing to start work on his third instructional book, reviewing some of the material before going into the studio the next day. What was needed, we agreed, were more useful movements in the basics and katas. We didn't want to keep the fighting techniques separate from the basic movements. They should be closer in practice, so beginning students learned early on the practical moves they would need in fighting stance. I told my teacher about the white belt at my dojo who kept doing his mawashi uke with his upper blocking hand outside the lower hand. Turned on a horizontal plane, the mawashi uke was more useful for blocking a punch and hooking the neck in a close-in fighting position, but only as the white belt had persisted—with the blocking hand in front.

My teacher agreed right away that it was a more natural movement, so we changed the mawashi uke right then and there. It turned out that this position was not only more natural, but more useful in blocking kicks as well.

This is a typical example of staying open to all possibilities. As soon as you start thinking in terms of roles—"I am the teacher, he is the student"—you stop learning. Never think you are above learning from a lower belt.

Consider the gedan barai. Traditionally this move was taught with the blocking hand coming down from the ear and parrying *from within* the front hand. Recently I changed the gedan barai to make it more practical; instead of pulling the blocking hand down from the *inside* of the protecting "up" hand, I now have it blocking down from *outside* the protecting hand. This block is usually taught from the inside, but it occurred to me that doing the block from the outside could be more effective. Don't be afraid to go against popular trends and try something different, especially if you know inside that it makes sense. If it doesn't work, you can always change back. The important thing is to keep looking for a better way of doing things.

A Sharpened Sword

Always try to polish your karate. You needn't show it off, but you must keep it sharp like a sword. That means keeping it up-to-date and practical. To my mind, "keeping sharp" means not only being in shape, but keeping your karate ultimately practical. It's not enough to train every day if the techniques you're training in are not useful. You may be in good shape, but your karate would be like drawing a rusty sword. Even if you can draw it quickly, it won't cut.

Strategy in Kumite and in Life

I developed a flexible fighting style out of necessity. As I prepared for the All-Japan in 1978, I reviewed tapes of my fights in the World Tournament three years previously and noticed that I had mostly used my hands. After throwing a punch, I rarely followed it with a kick or another combination. I knew that I wouldn't be able to stand toe to toe and exchange punches against a large fighter, like Nakamura in 1978. I would probably be outmuscled and pushed back as well, so I worked on my front kick in order to stop his forward momentum. That way I could create an opening for punches and kicks of my own. The strategy worked, and I was able to keep Nakamura off balance. It enabled me to knock him down once with a front kick and stun him with a roundhouse kick to the face.

To be the best fighter you can requires the ability to outwit your opponent. Read his strategy. Always look for patterns in his style or technique that you can use to your advantage. Kojiro Sasaki was Musashi Miyamoto's archenemy. He had the finest, most elegant technique of any swordsman in Japan, yet Musashi Miyamoto was able to defeat him with a bluntly carved oar and a sharper sense of strategy.

The strategies for kumite can be thought of as tactics for living as well. No matter how daunting, there is a way to face any challenge in life, just as there is a way to face any opponent in kumite.

In kumite a step back moves you out of range of attack and draws your opponent toward you. But too many steps backward and you are suddenly running away, and your opponent can easily knock you down. That's why it's important to set a limit. Counter within three steps back, and do so decisively without a thought for the consequences.

As in kumite, so in life. Decide ahead of time just how far you will step back from a challenge before you answer it decisively. This way there is no procrastinating or lack of resolve; you give yourself a timetable for action, and you stick to it. Maybe the first answer is wrong. Maybe you are pressed again. Three steps—see the situation and react. This way you are ready for every challenge.

If you face an opponent who moves, knock him down. If he doesn't move, knock him down. Otherwise your fighting will be vague and without purpose. The same is true in life; finish what you start. You have a responsibility to complete any challenge that you accept.

Never turn your back to an opponent. If you do, you expose yourself to injury. If you cannot see what is coming, you will never be able to counter it. Turning your back to any challenge is the same as giving up.

Spirit is the most important element in kumite, because it alone will take you into the moment and allow you to sense the rhythm and find the opening—*suki*—for any attack. Power can be defeated every time by strategy and technique, but you need the heart and spirit to stay calm. That way you can find a path into the eye of any storm, no matter how loudly it may roar.

You may knock down your opponent. You may be knocked down yourself. But either way, it is important to understand why. In the dojo, on the street, be curious and ask questions. You can learn nothing if you are proud or selfish, or think you know the answers. Find "how to die" so that your spirit can look directly into a problem and find the solution.

Lessons for the Mind

Yukichi Fukuzawa was a Japanese educator and founder of Keio University in Tokyo. He lived during the nineteenth century and played an important role in the development of Japanese society after the collapse of feudalism. Fukuzawa wrote a series of precepts entitled "Lessons for the Mind" that I have always treasured. In many ways these guidelines capture the essential qualities of budo. I keep them on the wall of my dojo:

The most splendid and enjoyable thing in this world is said to be having work one can do throughout one's life.

The most miserable thing for a human being in this world is to be without culture.

The most beautiful thing in this world is to have love and affection for all things.

The saddest thing in this world is telling lies.

The most disgraceful thing in this world is to envy another's livelihood.

The most precious thing in this world is doing for others without expecting to receive anything at all.

The loneliest thing in this world is to not have work to do.

Summer Camp Training

The dojo is a place away from the everyday world, away from the appointments and schedules of our daily business. But even in the dojo routine can become too familiar. Sometimes students need to step away from the dojo and train in a different setting. They need to discover a quiet place where they can reflect on their training. When I spent three weeks at Kawanohama Beach, I came back to the dojo with a fresh mind.

This is the value of summer camp training. In past years, during the summer I have tried to take my students to the mountains for three days of camp training. They eat, sleep, train, and relax together. Usually we choose a peaceful setting near a lake, a place that gives everyone a chance to look at himself and others in a different light. The roles and identities these students have assumed in the dojo take on a new dimension.

The training is important, but other experiences are equally valuable. Cooperating in preparing meals and cleaning up, learning to work together, and sharing responsibilities regardless of one's background, job, or income—these are the most valuable lessons. For three days everyone is the same, working and living together.

In the evening we gather around a campfire and entertain ourselves. Everyone is expected to stand up and perform. This in itself is a valuable experience because it reveals a different part of each student's personality and allows each one to feel accepted by the group no matter what the level

Summer Camp training, Horsetooth Reservoir, Colorado, 1998.

Punching sumo at Enshin summer camp training in Chiba, Japan, 1999.

of talent. They can stand up and sing or tell a joke, and they know they will be applauded no matter how embarrassing their performance. Even the shyest student is encouraged to stand up and perform, and generally does so because he knows he cannot fail in this group. For the performers, these moments on the stage are still another way of building confidence as the group shares in the acceptance of the individual. It offers the kind of acceptance you find only in a family.

Training at summer camp takes place on the beach or in the water. Students learn to carry the challenge out of the dojo and into any situation or environment. They understand that the wind, sand, and water each have something to teach. The foot pivots differently on sand than it does on hardwood. Executing a front kick against the resistance of water teaches something to the muscles they cannot know from working in thin air.

As Musashi said: *"Onore igai wa mina shinari"* ("Besides yourself, everything else is a teacher"). The black belt can learn from the white belt. A man can learn strategy from a mongoose. Even the elements have lessons to teach if we stay open to them.

During summer camp training I always find it interesting to observe the adjustments that lower belts make as they take their karate into a new setting; you can almost see their minds working. For example, at first there is always the awkward feeling of training on a beach in front of strangers. From this, students learn that self-consciousness is just a thought, which, like other thoughts, will pass away when they give themselves to their kicks and punches.

It is similar to taking a group downtown at lunchtime to put on a demonstration promoting a tournament or school. The new ones always feel out of place at first. It is usually at these demonstrations that I ask students to perform a breaking technique. We do not practice these breaks in the dojo; they are only done at demonstrations, and generally the students don't know they will be asked to perform a break until I call them out from the group.

I never ask students to break more than I already know they're capable of doing. Most accept this challenge without another thought. They focus on the task at hand and let their fears evaporate.

It is a valuable experience to attempt a break in front of strangers—even failing is important and worthwhile. In the long run, the experience reduces the fear of failing; if you are always afraid of failure, you will never try anything. Success, of course, builds confidence and provides a higher goal for next time. But the important thing is not success or failure, but the doing. The process counts more than the result; putting yourself through the challenge and observing yourself respond to that challenge matters more than the external judgment of how you performed. This is the essence of karate, the heart of its process . . . learning to face challenge in a controlled manner.

Tournaments

The year I won the All-Japan I organized my first full-contact tournament in Denver. I rented a high school gymnasium, set up a single-elimination pyramid for sixteen fighters, and eight hundred people showed up. What they saw was a full-contact karate tournament—no pads, no gloves—open to all styles. A lot of people told me I was crazy to try to build this kind of tournament. They said Americans wouldn't come to watch and that fighters would think it was too rough. But I believed in the tournament because it was the fairest and most demanding test of karate skills I had seen. For this reason, I knew it would succeed.

It took years of hard work, but the Sabaki Challenge Tournament grew year by year. We moved from the high school to a college arena, to the Denver Coliseum, and eventually into McNichols Arena, where we hosted 32 fighters and 7500 spectators in 1995. With the advent of two more professional sports franchises here in Denver (baseball and hockey), the competition increased and our audience gradually decreased, but the tournament's spirit and dedication have remained the same. In 1999 we held the Sabaki Challenge at Boettcher Concert Hall in the Denver Performing Arts Complex—a wonderful venue, in the round, with excellent seating in all locations. In addition to our three weight divisions, in the last two years we have opened the tournament to women, who compete in an open division. The women compete under exactly the same rules as the men, and their matches have provided some of the most spirited fights of the tournament. The Sabaki Challenge continues to draw top karate fighters in all styles from around the country and abroad.

In 1989 *Black Belt Magazine* called the Sabaki Challenge "the most popular single-day martial arts event in the country." Ten years later *Black Belt* wrote that the Sabaki Challenge "has set the standard for bare-knuckled full-contact competition in the U.S."

Our Sabaki Challenge videos continue to capture the fighting action with "live call" and color commentary explaining the strategies, techniques, and styles of the various

The stage was set for the 1992 Sabaki Challenge at Mammoth Events Center, Denver, Colorado.

Koichi Ninomiya performing a side kick during the children's demonstration at the 1994 Sabaki Challenge.

*My demonstration with Sensei John Arnold
at the 1994 Sabaki Challenge.*

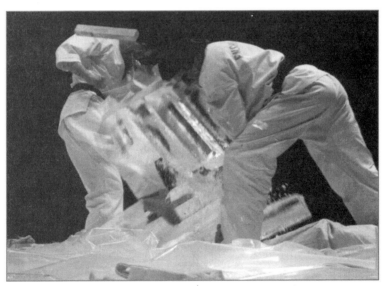

Breaking ice with a shin kick at the '94 Sabaki Challenge.

competitors. Since our first video in 1989, the "voice" of the Sabaki Challenge has been Michael Klahr. A former sport-stalk radio host and martial artist, Michael is knowledgeable about karate and boxing alike. His exhaustive Sabaki preparation includes fighter interviews that bring out the human stories behind the competition. Michael has been a wonderful performer and a good friend to the Sabaki Challenge.

The Sabaki Challenge videos have aired on regional cable networks to an audience of fifteen million around the country. They are available for purchase through our Web site or headquarters. Whether the Sabaki Challenge attracts 750 or 7500, I promise that it will continue to offer the highest quality full-contact kumite there is.

One of the reasons I started organizing a tournament was to provide a test for some of my more competitive students, a way for them to measure themselves against fighters from other styles. Although I had been guilty of "dojo bashing" as a young man, I didn't encourage it in my own students. If my own students wanted to build their confidence by facing students in other styles, I wanted to provide a forum in which to do it safely and with respect. Furthermore, tournament competition had been a large part of my own background in karate. Although I had left it at the top to broaden my own horizons within karate, I still saw the value of tournament competition.

I had always dreamed of building a major tournament that would draw fighters from around the world, similar to the All-Japan in which I had fought so many times: full-contact, knockdown karate. But unlike the All-Japan, I wanted to stress technique as well as spirit.

I do not expect all of my students to compete in the Sabaki Challenge—far from it. The tournament is only for those who wish to take their training a few steps further. I emphasize that the goal in this competition is the personal challenge; winning is almost beside the point. Those who compete must look to push themselves a little further, to improve their technique, to build their spirit and challenge themselves beyond their normal limits in the dojo. This is the value of tournament competition. A fighter's preparation and the way he carries himself during the competition . . . these are the most important concerns—not who wins or loses.

Today the Sabaki Challenge is a national event and continues to grow in popularity. Although it is no longer the only tournament featuring real fighting karate without pads or gloves, its emphasis on both strength *and* technique makes its format one of the most demanding I can think of. A fighter cannot simply "show up" for this tournament; he must prepare.

For spectators a tournament is always like an iceberg. They see only the event itself—they don't see the hours and months of fighter preparation that preceded it. It takes total commitment to ready oneself for a competition that may require the entrant to face three different fighters in one evening to get to the top of a division.

Over the years I have refined the rules for the Sabaki Challenge in order to emphasize technique as well as power and spirit. The old full-contact tournaments were displays of raw spirit only: two fighters squared off and exchanged numerous punches to the chest. If an opening presented itself, you tried to land a roundhouse kick. The only way to score points was by knocking out your opponent with a roundhouse kick.

This kind of fighting seems unrealistic to me, because out on the street, if your opponent has a knife, you can't afford to take repeated blows. You must move outside and counter quickly or else lose your life. That is why I started to award points for sweeps and throws. If an opponent is doubled over by a punch or momentarily stunned by a kick, these techniques earn points. If fighters can score with stunning kicks and punches that cause an opponent to turn away momentarily, they will have to be prepared to use technique rather than power alone to defend and attack.

Furthermore, in many tournaments, I've seen champions swept to the mat or thrown without their opponents being awarded points. In other cases I've seen champions swept, but because their attacker didn't follow with a controlled punch, no points were allowed. This too seems unfair. If you can take an opponent down with a sweep, you deserve to score. That's why Sabaki rules reward points for sweeps and throws whether they're followed by a controlled punch or not. Overall, these rules make for a more realistic test of fighting skills.

Here's a breakdown of scoring rules and penalties for the Sabaki Challenge:

✳ In order to win, a fighter must be the first to score six points. In the case of a tie, a winner is awarded the decision by the judges and referee on the basis of technique and spirit.

✳ A blow forcing the defender to turn away will be scored as one point.

✳ A throwing or sweeping takedown, when the attacker stays on his feet but does not follow immediately with a controlled punch or kick, scores one point.

* A single sweep or throwing technique followed by a controlled punch or kick scores three points.

* Any technique that doubles over the opponent scores three points.

* Any blow that downs an opponent so his hand and hip or hand and knee touch the mat scores three points.

* A knockout scores six points and is an automatic victory. (A knockout occurs when a fighter is legally downed and is unable to rise before five seconds.)

Techniques that are *not* allowed include face punches, elbow strikes to the face, groin kicks, and encircling the opponent's body or neck with both hands.

The Sabaki Challenge uses a cumulative system of warnings and penalties. Lesser offenses like holding, grabbing, groin kicks, or running out of the fighting area constitute a warning. The first three warnings constitute a penalty. The next two warnings constitute a second penalty. And the final warning or penalty results in disqualification. Penalties are levied for face punches, direct kicks to the front of the knee, or when a fighter makes full contact with a strike or kick after his opponent is down. Two face punches result in immediate disqualification.

Of all the students training in my dojo, only a handful end up fighting in the tournament. Regular training in the dojo is very different, of course, from what goes on in one of my tournaments. The tournament is only for those few competitors who are willing to make the commitment. For them it means months of extra training to acquire the necessary conditioning and strength. The techniques are no different from those learned in a normal training session in the dojo, but the sessions are more intensive.

In the dojo we emphasize technique above power and speed, because not everyone wants to make a career of fighting tournaments. Students all have different goals. Perhaps some want to fight tournaments, but others are there to learn self-defense, lose weight, or build self-confidence. Unlike the tournament, training in the dojo provides a way to reach those goals. In this sense, I've always believed the dojo should be for everyone—men, women, and children—no matter what their age or ability.

There are no yardsticks in karate. The color of a belt means very little, because the only real measure of one's progress is internal. Whether it is in a tournament or the dojo, the important measure is how far a student or a fighter can take him or herself. It is the process itself and not the result that matters.

Sports in this country are designed first to measure achievement and second, spirit or character. Even on an amateur level, young people are constantly groomed to win a trophy or a national ranking. Very rarely do young people train for the sense of self-discovery and personal growth their sport has to offer. Effort attached to success and money may be a stimulant for achievement, but one has to wonder what the true content of that achievement is, once the money and trophies no longer come.

What is easy for one student to achieve may be hard for another. One student may be strong and coordinated, another weak and stiff. It may be easier for one to earn a black belt and quite hard for the other. But what counts most is not the belt. It is not the achievement itself, but the level of effort that goes into that achievement. For this reason I tell students, whether they are working in the dojo or fighting in a tournament, that they are not competing against each other, but only against themselves. This is a message that they can carry into the workplace or onto the tournament mat.

Some of my younger students may carry this lesson back into the classroom. An A in English may be a snap for one student but difficult for another. Ultimately what matters is what you learn, not the grade. In an educational system that awards grades and demands higher and higher results, this is easily forgotten.

In order to stay involved with the "process" in school, at work, or in the dojo, it is important not to set unrealistic goals. Don't aim too high, because if your goals are unreachable, you will only defeat yourself; your attempt will be little more than a self-fulfilling prophecy of failure. But if you look only as far as the task at hand—taking things a moment at a time—then the job is manageable.

For example, if you're fighting in a tournament and have an easy first-round draw, don't think beyond that opponent, or he will invariably surprise you. By the same logic, if you're a white belt thinking only of earning your black belt, you will not pay attention to the basic techniques you need to learn in order to lay the foundation. I often see ambitious lower belts rush through their combinations to prove they know the sequence, only to sacrifice their technique for each punch or kick. If you're busy comparing yourself with the black belts, you will always feel inadequate. Pay attention to the task at hand. Give effort to what can be done, not to the things that are out of reach. Learn to walk before you try to run.

I recall one fighter in a recent tournament who was in too much of a hurry. He was a strong lightweight who had trained hard for months in preparation and couldn't wait to get onto the mat. In the first round of the tournament, all fighters are required to break three boards with a knife edge or fist strike. This particular fighter came jogging out, eager to get on with his match. In a blur he broke the required three boards with a knife hand and jumped up ready to begin.

During his match he fought aggressively and defeated his opponent, but toward the end of the round I noticed that he wasn't using his right hand; it had swollen considerably. After the match the doctor examined him; his hand was fractured. Later he admitted that he had rushed his breaking technique and had caught the boards at the wrong angle. He hadn't given his full attention. It was unfortunate, but at least he had learned the importance of shoshin—keeping the mind fresh and focused on the moment instead of looking too far ahead. It is a very common mistake and often a painful lesson to learn. If it can be learned without injury, that is better still; but all too often injury is the body's way of reminding us to concentrate.

This same Japanese fighter competed four times in the Sabaki Challenge. His first three appearances, though spirited, were unsuccessful. He was impatient and in poor condition mentally. His training was inconsistent. He had energy but lacked focus. After his third attempt he was resolved to win at all costs. If a broken hand had taught him the importance of shoshin—focus—he wanted to make sure he stayed focused in preparation for the next Sabaki Challenge.

When he first came to the United States three years earlier, he had introduced himself to me, explaining that we had already met once before—soon after I had won the All-Japan, at an autograph session in Osaka. He said he had waited in line for two hours to meet me because I was like a god to him. Although his parents had hoped he would go to medical school, he moved to the United States instead, in order to pursue his dream of teaching karate. He was going to school and running a dojo in Wyoming. On his vacations he would drive down to Denver and train at my dojo.

The year before the 1989 tournament this young man moved to Boulder, and that was when he came to me and told me about his goal of winning the Sabaki Challenge. He said he wanted to dedicate himself to that one goal and asked if he could live with me and train every day.

I was surprised at this request. In those days this fighter was living a loose lifestyle, and I questioned whether he would have the determination to stay with a tough training regimen. He explained to me that his mother had recently come for a visit from Japan. She told him that she was concerned about his lifestyle. She cried in front of him and whispered that she worried he was wasting his life. Perhaps he wanted to prove that he wasn't.

In November of 1988 my fast-paced friend moved in to the dormitory next to my living quarters at the dojo. He got up and ran and bag-trained with me each morning. He had been working nights as a hibachi chef at a popular Japanese restaurant in Boulder, and he kept his job, commuting from my dojo every day by bus—a trip that took an hour and a half each way. He helped with chores around the dojo and dormitory, He cooked and cleaned. And he trained, morning and afternoon.

When the young man's mother came back for another visit shortly before the tournament, she was happily surprised. Afterward she me wrote me a lengthy letter saying she could tell from her son's eyes that he was making something of himself. He had written her that he knew he would do anything in order to train with me.

As a hibachi chef, my young friend was often toasted with drink by his customers, and they often bought him sake to show their appreciation of his quick knife and gracious manner. One night he arrived home after too much "appreciation" and fell asleep under my kitchen table. He was too drunk to move. He slept there the rest of the night, but the next morning, bright and early, he was up for training. For that one year, he trained harder than any student I have ever had. No matter how little sleep he'd had the night before, no matter what the weather—rain or snow—he was up and running every morning.

We worked hard on my young friend's technique that year. He had a bad habit of pulling his head away from an oncoming attack instead of staying set and blocking the blow with his hands. I got him to hold still and stay poised for a block and counter. We refined many of his techniques, but my last piece of advice to him before the tournament was to use his left hand for his breaking technique. I had done this myself in the All-Japan. Both hands are important during kumite, but the right is the power hand. It isn't worth taking chances on an injury before the fight has even started.

My live-in student went on to win the Sabaki Challenge in convincing fashion. He knocked out his first opponent and defeated the next two on points, using crisp sweeping techniques. His conditioning was excellent. He was patient in looking for his openings and his eyes were focused with a clarity and intensity that burned cleanly into the moment.

Today Nobuhiko Kishi is one of my top instructors. He runs his own Enshin school in Boulder, where he has trained many Sabaki Challenge champions.

Nobuhiko Kishi in the finals of the '89 Sabaki Challenge.

Another young fighter embodied still a different lesson about the importance of using one's head as well as one's body and spirit.

He was a tall, handsome, muscular fighter with great strength and a powerful spirit. He fought like a wild animal but unfortunately paid little attention to the rules. As I said, in my tournament I developed a set of rules that reward technique as well as power and speed—a way of protecting the fighters and bringing out the strategy of kumite. These rules clearly prohibit any punches or hand strikes to the face. Kicks are allowed to the head, but punches to the head are penalized: two face punches and a fighter is disqualified.

The fighters all knew these rules; they had been explained in detail through our correspondence and at a demonstration meeting the night before the tournament.

All the same, "wild man" could not remember to keep his punches down. As strong as he was, he wasn't strong enough to control his own punches. Too often he hit his opponent in the face and raised a lump under his eye. It was a close fight, and he might have been able to win if he had stayed within the rules. But he didn't, and the judges disqualified him.

It is important not only to have a strong body and spirit; one must also have a strong mind and be able to adapt to the situation at hand. It takes intelligence to know the rules and adapt your strengths accordingly. In business, in life, in karate, this is an important secret of success.

A sense of balance is important, especially where the body, spirit, and mind are concerned. Unlike the young fighter who didn't use his mind enough, another fighter used his intellect too much. He confused the fighting he did in his head with what he should have been doing on the mat.

In preparing for the tournament, this fellow watched videotapes of other fighters in his division, talking about techniques and strategy. When he learned who his first-round draw would be, he spent hours going over footage from that fighter's previous tournament. He too had come to my dojo several weeks before the tournament to train with me. But often he didn't show up for training. He would sleep late and skip his running, or he would show up late and work halfheartedly. I knew that if he continued to get his training from a videotape instead of putting time in at the dojo, he was heading for trouble.

At the tournament he fought hard but lost his first-round match. Later he explained to everyone that he had actually fought a brilliant fight; he was still talking a good game. But some students learn from their mistakes, and others refuse. This fellow believed he had prepared himself solidly and probably will never be convinced otherwise. The lesson is clear: It pays to do your training in the dojo instead of in your head.

A large tournament brings many different kinds of people together from around the country and around the world. But as different as these competitors may be in style or personality, they all share a common interest. Whatever the individual failings, there is always a positive spirit, and the greatest reward for me in the Sabaki Challenge is the fellowship and mutual respect the fighters show one another during the competition and afterward.

The mat is like a crucible. A match is a trial by fire. And to have gone through that challenge creates a bond between fighters. They may start as rivals, but they end up as brothers.

All of the fighters who participate in the Sabaki Challenge carry with them a spirit of budo. It is an unspoken code. They conduct themselves in a manner that is quiet and humble. They come to fight with an open heart, ready to learn from their experience. They have come not only to learn new moves or techniques, but because they are committed to learning something more about themselves as well. Take, for example, the burly heavyweight from Nebraska, his massive arms covered with tattoos. After he lost his first-round fight, he came up to me and said, "This was the best tournament I've ever participated in. I can't wait to come back and try again next year."

Goals

People with their minds set on reaching a goal may often look foolish to others because they concentrate so hard on one thing. But when that inventor or explorer has reached his goal and turns out to be a Thomas Edison or a Marco Polo, suddenly he is no longer a fool but a genius.

When I lived in Matsuyama after leaving the Goyo Construction Company, I had little money, a tiny apartment with no toilet, and a simple diet of ramen and rice. Things seemed very hard indeed, and people probably thought I was foolish for concentrating so single-mindedly on winning the All-Japan.

As the saying goes, "You can drink sake, but don't let the sake drink you."

As a young man I was lucky in this regard: I was allergic to drink (and still am). I didn't gamble. And, as Kancho said, I had a funny face that scared away the girls. It was just as well—this enabled me to concentrate on reaching my goals and to keep setting new ones so that I didn't become too smug or self-satisfied.

Success does not come to everyone at the same stage in life. So don't be discouraged if you don't succeed early. If you work hard and take longer to achieve your goals, the rewards are even greater. Success is kindest to those who work longest. The twenty-year-old flash is soon forgotten.

Training in Honbu.

The dojo is a microcosm of the world outside. Your attitudes and feelings in the dojo tell everything about your behavior outside as well. Training at summer camp, Ehime, Japan.

In and Out of the Dojo

The dojo is a microcosm of the world outside. Your attitudes and feelings in the dojo tell everything about your behavior outside as well. For example, if you are sloppy about the way you care for your gi, then you are probably sloppy about your technique, your job, and many other matters in both the dojo and in life.

Just as the dojo reflects the world outside, so the body is a mirror of the mind. The way a person carries himself tells much about the health of his state of mind. So many people we pass on the street walk without any awareness of their bodies. Their backs are hunched and their shoulders stooped as if they carried the weight of the world on their shoulders. If they would only "empty their hands," much of that burden would drop away.

Musashi Miyamoto was the best kind of figure for his time, but he may not be a good example for living today. The world is different from what it was in Musashi's time. It is harder, for example, to achieve the best and follow budo with a wife and family. But this is a condition of so many people's lives today, so it is important to try. To take the spirit of karate out of the dojo and apply its principles to your relationships with those around you—family, friends, neighbors—is an even greater challenge than living those ideals in isolation. This should be the goal for today's Musashi.

Setting an Example

The top students in any dojo show all there is to know about a given school. They are the proof of what that style will bring. Their leadership and example is extremely important because karate is taught by example from the top down, and students at the bottom inevitably emulate the models they have before them.

In my dojo I have always emphasized technique and philosophy. I started out training for the All-Japan. I know the feeling of competition and long hours of training. But I left competition to explore karate's inner values as well. As a teacher, I believe it is important to stress both sides, and this is best done by example. It is not enough to talk philosophy or during training leave the teaching to your black belts.

Both the practical and philosophical aspects of karate are important. But they must be kept in balance, and the best way to keep that balance—whether as teacher or student—is to do as much as you can within the dojo.

I try to pass on this sense of balance to my top students, some of whom have gone on to open schools of their own. This leadership is the heart of a style.

If the top students don't use control and end up intimidating the lower belts, then those actions will infect the school. If upper belts don't come to training, it says something else about your school. If they don't show respect, or don't keep themselves or the dojo clean, that also reflects badly.

I have been fortunate to have a strong core of very solid san-dans and *yon-dans* (fourth-degree black belts), but there are several who deserve special mention for their effort and leadership in the dojo almost since my very first days in Denver. They are Joel Humphrey, Vernon Owens, and Don Doubleday. These students have formed the core of my group in Denver, and they have been with me through thick and thin. I continue to look to their leadership in the dojo to help pass on my techniques and ideals. Their loyalty and spirit have been a great encouragement to me over the years.

As Enshin karate continues to grow in popularity, I look to new leadership to help carry the responsibility of passing on my technique and ideas. In addition to existing Enshin schools around the country, new schools are springing up in Japan, England, Germany, South Africa, Peru, and Chile.

I never planned to have a large network of schools; it just happened over the years. But in spite of our growth, I am still determined to oversee each school personally and maintain a high quality of karate. I refuse to give away black belt degrees or confer territory simply for the sake of opening new schools. Karate must come first.

In order for an instructor to join Enshin karate, he must come to Denver and train with me personally to learn the techniques firsthand and to get a feel for the relationship I encourage between myself and my students. I believe strongly in personal contact with instructors, and I will travel to their dojos to teach and oversee promotion tests. I look first for quality, not quantity. At Enshin karate, the door is open to instructors from other styles; but new instructors must enter knowing I expect dedication and hard work. To those who have been with me for some time, I am prepared to delegate even greater responsibilities.

As an example of the *wrong* kind of candidate, let me tell the story of a man whom I will call Mr. Business. Mr. Business was a karate instructor in a large eastern city who was interested in our style. Over the phone he sounded enthusiastic and eager to learn our new techniques. He brought me to his city, put me in a nice hotel, and arranged to have me perform a demonstration for his students.

I could see from his dojo that Mr. Business was very efficient; he charged his students to the penny and ran a very strict school. After talking over arrangements in his office, Mr. Business agreed to come to Denver to study with me, but I knew something was wrong when I went into the dojo to start my demonstration and Mr. Business was nowhere to be found.

Later that night on the way to dinner, he apologized lightly for having missed my demonstration. It wasn't important for him to be at my demonstration, he explained, because he had been studying martial arts for thirty years and could learn my techniques in just a few minutes. Then he asked if I intended to give him control of the whole state. It was clear by then that Mr. Business had very little interest in my karate. For him it was only dollars and cents. We decided it would be best for both of us if we went our separate ways.

I believe communication with all the schools in my network is very important. Newsletters, kata sheets, instructor's tapes—these are all ways of keeping teachers and students up-to-date. The person responsible for coordinating all communication with the other schools is my chief administrator, Nancy Zorensky.

A san-dan, Nancy has helped organize Enshin karate and is responsible for much of the correspondence, mailing lists, and information sheets that keep our organization running smoothly. Without Nancy's help I would not be able to stay as closely in touch with the other Enshin schools as I do

Nancy Zorensky has been the administrator for Enshin Karate and the Sabaki Challenge for thirteen years. Ed and Nancy have worked with me on numerous projects.

now. Nancy has also coordinated preparations for the Sabaki Challenge and has helped make the tournament so successful over the years. In addition to her work with me, she and her husband Ed operated an Enshin dojo in southeast Denver for eleven years.

Another student who has gone on to open his own school is Vernon Owens. Vernon trained with me in Denver and went on to teach Enshin karate in Fulda, Germany, where he was stationed with the army.

At the age of 31 when he returned from the service, Vernon came to Denver to fight in the 1990 Sabaki Challenge as a middleweight. After a six-year layoff from tournament competition, Vernon came back in fine style. His technique was sharp and his speed was better than ever. I can still picture the lightning quickness of Vernon's roundhouse kick, which knocked out a tough Canadian fighter, Norm Rivard, in the first eleven seconds of their final-round match.

Today Vernon runs a strong dojo in Seattle and hosts his own Sabaki satellite tournament, the Great Northwest Sabaki. Karate remains an important part of Vernon's life. He is a worthy champion and a fine example of Enshin spirit.

For several years Brett Layser was an Enshin instructor at my Boulder branch. An excellent student, Brett also came back to Denver to compete in the '90 Sabaki Challenge after a year in the marines. At the time Brett was stationed in Florida, training to be a pilot. In fact, while bag-training in a gym down there shortly before the tournament, Brett was approached by two bystanders who asked if he had ever heard of the Sabaki Challenge. "Heard of it?" he answered.

Brett Layser in action from the 1991 Sabaki Challenge.

"I've won the lightweight title once and I'm training to win it a second time!"

At 148 pounds, Brett was small but powerful. An excellent technician, he developed a strong fighting style in which he pulled down his opponent's lead arm and attacked the head with high roundhouse kicks. He was adaptive and smart at finding his openings. When opponents caught on to his favorite attack and raised their hands to protect the face, Brett attacked the body instead. Brett scored a decision and two knockouts on his way to a second lightweight title, and he did it with a clinic-like display of Sabaki technique.

Nineteen years ago a student came from Japan and studied with me for one year. Small in stature but big of heart,

Small in stature but big of heart, Yasuhiko Nakano set a strong example in the dojo. On my visit to Peru in 1997, at Machupic-chu in Peru with Sensei Nakano and his student Henry.

Yasuhiko Nakano set a strong example in the dojo; he never once missed a training session. Nakano has since moved to Peru, where he has opened an Enshin dojo in the city of Tacna. Starting a dojo in a poor country is a challenge that typifies Nakano's dedication and spirit. He once told me that if it took me ten years to establish Enshin in the United States, he was determined to build Enshin in Peru, even if it took him twenty years.

In 1990 Nakano came to Denver to fight in the Sabaki Challenge. Matched against larger fighters, he impressed the judges and audience alike with his fighting spirit. Today his dojo continues to thrive in Tacna. He holds an annual Sabaki satellite tournament each year, and brings the winner to compete in the Sabaki Challenge.

I already mentioned the man who so admired my performance in winning the 1978 All-Japan that he named his child for me. Koji Masuda, of Chiba, Japan, had been training in karate for quite a few years when I started Enshin karate. A short time later he came to the United States to train and talk about opening his own branch. Today Masuda remains a serious student of karate and an excellent teacher. A man of great warmth, both generous and helpful, he runs the Enshin network of schools in Japan. We visit frequently in Chiba and at other Enshin schools throughout the country. He regularly attends the Sabaki Challenge here in Denver. I have enjoyed watching Masuda's family grow over the years, especially his son, now twenty, Joko Masuda—my namesake.

There are many top students who have continued to train with me over the years and have helped me in various ways, according to their own skills. Many of these men and women are listed in the dedication at the front of the book. Whether it has been helping to organize the tournament, putting on demonstrations, or refurbishing the dojo, these students have always been there to lend a hand and serve as examples to the lower belts. These accomplishments are not mine alone. We all share in them together. This is the spirit of Enshin.

Each one of us can be a winner. We each may start at a different age or with a different level of ability. But what is most important is how far you can go, not how quickly you achieve results. Here are a few examples of special students and teachers, whom I consider remarkable for bringing a special attitude to their training, regardless of the obstacles standing in their way.

Michael Miles

Almost twenty-five years ago, Michael Miles was in a serious car accident that left him paralyzed from the waist down and with limited use of his arms and hands. In the years that followed he met with countless setbacks and hurdles in his effort to pull his life together in both mind and spirit.

In 1989 Michael started to train in Enshin Karate with Sensei Ed Zorensky, who developed a special training program tailored specifically for Michael's disability. With regular workouts Michael got stronger and the mobility in his arms improved. After two years, Michael moved downtown and continued his training with me at the *honbu*. I became more and more aware of the extraordinary courage and spirit Michael brought to everything he did. In 1995, after earning his black belt, Michael was featured in an inspiring demonstration at the Sabaki Challenge. It was a high point for Michael in his training, but a short time later he received

A demonstration featuring Michael Miles at the 1994 Sabaki Challenge at McNichols Arena, in Denver.

devastating news; his doctors told him that he had developed bone cancer and they would have to amputate his right leg from the knee down. Three weeks later Michael called to say that he was ready to come back to training. Most people would have given up after a setback like this, but not Michael. He has been through numerous infections and illnesses, but each time he comes back to continue his training. We think of karate as a struggle against an opponent, but in life very often the greatest opponent is within. Michael has faced these inner challenges many times and has always returned with a positive spirit and strong will.

In 1999 Michael again provided a dramatic display of Sabaki technique at the tournament, including a double break with a knife hand and elbow strike. At the end of his demonstration I awarded Michael his second-degree black belt, and he received a standing ovation. There are few students who have taught me as much about courage and spirit as Michael Miles. He may not compete in the Sabaki Challenge, but Michael is unquestionably a champion in life.

Paden Wolfe

Starting his training in Enshin as an undergraduate at the University of Colorado, Paden showed up consistently for class and worked quietly at improving every aspect of his fighting. Paden was not flashy, fast, or overwhelmingly strong; he was a skinny undergraduate with a keen ability to work hard and stay focused. As time passed Paden became stronger and quicker. He decided to test himself by fighting in the Sabaki Challenge as a lightweight. His first year he showed terrific spirit; although he lost in the finals, he was awarded the Sabaki Spirit trophy.

The next year, in 1994, Paden competed again and used an aggressive attacking style to win the lightweight division. Seeking another challenge, Paden decided the following year to compete as a middleweight. He ended up facing Hideto Otsu, the 1993 Lightweight Champion who had defeated him in the finals—the only man to win the Sabaki Challenge in two weight divisions. Paden defeated Otsu and became the 1995 Middleweight Champion. Still eager to challenge himself, the next year Paden moved up to the heavyweight division. He lost in the semifinals to a man who outweighed him by fifty pounds.

As a young man, Paden started at the bottom of the mountain; methodically, he kept working his way up until he

*Paden Wolfe started at the bottom of the mountain
and methodically kept working his way up until he
eventually became a champion in two divisions.
Paden scoring a takedown in the 1994 Sabaki Challenge.*

eventually became a champion in two divisions. His determination exemplified the old adage that "a steady drip of water over time will wear a hole even through stone."

Even though he didn't realize his goal of winning the heavyweight division, Paden gave it his best effort. If you set a goal and give 150 percent, even if you fail to reach that goal, you will feel confirmed in knowing that you have given your best effort. This is not a defeat. Although he lost his heavyweight challenge, Paden had the satisfaction of knowing that he had given his complete effort. Very often this is the greatest satisfaction you can have.

Today Sensei Paden Wolfe runs the Denver southeast dojo along with Sensei Frank Nafe. Retired from competition, Paden provides the color commentary for our Sabaki Challenge videos. With his broad experience in competition, he brings keen insight to these tapes. Paden continues to embody the spirit of Enshin.

Noboru Hino

At fifty-one years of age, Noboru Hino has been training in karate for twenty-eight years. Although he and I were from the same prefecture—Ehime—and had trained and taught under the same teacher, we never met until twelve years ago. At that time Mr. Hino ran a successful dojo with many black belts; but, due to a conflict with his organization, he felt compelled to leave his old style and closed his dojo. A year later his students urged him to reopen his school and continue training them. Mr. Hino felt that it was too large a responsibility for him to take on alone, without affiliation to a style or organization. He was also severely hampered by back and knee pain from old injuries, and didn't feel up to the task. He came to me to discuss the possibility of becoming part of the Enshin network in Japan; he told me about his reservations, and described his students' eagerness to have him back in the dojo. I told him to talk to Mr. Koji Masuda, my chief instructor for Japan.

With great anxiety Mr. Hino went to Chiba to meet with Mr. Masuda at his dojo. He was worried that he would encounter a gruff, militaristic karate sensei, who had little patience or concern for his problems. Arriving by train on a cold winter afternoon, Mr. Hino was wondering how to find his way to the dojo, when he spotted a man standing alone on the snowy platform. As he got off the train, the man stepped up and warmly welcomed him to Chiba: it was Mr. Masuda. From that moment, Mr. Hino felt at home with Enshin.

Eight years later Mr. Hino had developed ten Enshin schools with 300 students. Although he had been very successful in organizing and directing Enshin programs

At the grand opening of Mr. Koji Masuda's new dojo in Chiba, Japan, 1999. Mr. Masuda is sitting on my right. To his right, Mr. Noboru Hino.

throughout Ehime, his own physical condition had continued to deteriorate. He was in constant pain, and although he had tried many types of therapy, nothing seemed to help. A year ago, after the Sabaki Challenge, Mr. Hino came to me; he confessed that he felt he was holding back his students and instructors and had become a liability to the organization. He said he felt self-conscious that he could not train with his students or take part in the seminars and summer camp training with other instructors. No longer able to set a physical example for others in the dojo, he was convinced that he was of little use as an instructor. He was ready to quit Enshin and turn his schools over to his upper belts.

I told Mr. Hino that everyone gets old; everyone has injuries or infirmities that may not always be apparent. I explained that at those times when we suffer injuries, our students are looking at us most closely to see how we deal with the challenge. This is especially true as we get older. "Teaching karate is not just showing technique," I said. "What you show with your mind and spirit is as important as what you can show with your body. This is what it means to be a leader."

I reassured Mr. Hino that, ever since joining my organization almost ten years ago, he had set a strong example not only for his own students, but other instructors as well. I told him he had too much to offer to think of quitting now.

Mr. Hino was profoundly moved by my words; I could see the tears forming in his eyes. "I am 50 years old," he said. "I'm too old to be crying." Mr. Masuda, who had joined us, was also weeping.

A few months later I was in Japan, and attended a party celebrating Mr. Hino's tenth anniversary of teaching Enshin karate. As his top instructors stood up and offered toasts in his honor, one of them raised his glass and said, "Sensei Hino, you will always be our teacher. Even if you are in a wheelchair, I would be happy to push that chair to any dojo in Ehime just to have you teaching us."

I could see firsthand the love and appreciation Mr. Hino's students felt for him. I knew his decision to continue teaching had been the right one for everyone.

Sensei Nobuyuki Kishi

My mentor for the last twenty-five years has been Sensei Nobuyuki Kishi. He is an unusual man for our times, because he is totally unconcerned with material possessions and totally committed to his art—karate. His attitude to karate is embodied by a relentless search for the best way to fight against any opponent. Thinking about karate—*kyudoshin*—consumes his every waking moment. When we first met in New York, Mr. Kishi was my senpai. He has since gone on to develop his own style called Kishi Karate. I refer to him now as Sensei Kishi

A story about Sensei Kishi illustrates his keen sense of observation. He was walking down the street in Japan one day, when a group of rowdy college students approached from the opposite direction, pushing everyone out of their way. Determined not to be bullied, Sensei Kishi sized up the leader of the group, a very tall, long-haired lout, who seemed even taller in his fashionable high *getas* (Japanese high formal sandals made of wood), which clicked on the pavement with every step. As the students came to within a few feet of Sensei Kishi, the leader ordered Sensei Kishi off the street, or else. Seizing on the leader's most evident weakness, Sensei Kishi rushed forward and swept the fellow off his getas, leaving him in a heap in the middle of the street. The others ran off, and Sensei Kishi continued on his way as if nothing had happened.

In a street fight, Sensei Kishi always says there is no information, only quick judgments. Because each situation is

Sensei Nobuyuki Kishi and I sing Sakura Bana. After 25 years, we are still the closest of friends.

unique, you must size up your opponent quickly: his clothes, build, shoes—anything you can use to your advantage. If your opponent is wearing dress shoes with slippery soles, then use them to take him off balance. Expect everything, and learn as much as you can by watching.

Sensei Kishi talks often about preparing the mind before you encounter an opponent. He urges connecting to your opponent by going into his mind. This is very basic to karate, more basic than technique or power. Don't look ahead, anticipating the result; see the process. This is the essence of Kishi Karate, and sound advice for every encounter in life.

Not too long ago I visited Sensei Kishi in his home town of Yamagata in the north of Japan. We sat down to talk about the path of budo. Here is that conversation.

The Path to Budo Springs from Weakness

Sensei Kishi: Some people say that when the body starts to become weak, it becomes useless: "I'm too old, so I'll quit practicing." That thought comes easily as we get older. But I believe that budo springs from a feeling of weakness. People who practice martial arts begin to do so because they sense a weakness in themselves. Why then would you quit because you are weak or are growing old? The lesson that the martial arts teach is to overcome these weaknesses and continue on the path to self-improvement.

Kancho Ninomiya: I really believe this is true. Most people train hard only in their youth. They train for a tournament or a short-term goal, and once they've reached their goal they stop. Maybe you can call that "karate," but it is not the true meaning of budo. That is simply martial art techniques vs. the Way of Martial Arts. Continuing all of your life, that is the Way.

Sensei Kishi: Improving your health, overcoming shyness, seeking a way to work through hard times, bettering your life: these are all reasons why people start to practice martial arts. These reasons stem from weaknesses that people want to overcome. If you look at it this way, some of the qualifications that a martial artist must have are to be weak, afraid, cautious, and selfish. Everyone who looks at martial artists thinks that they are strong and brave, but these people started training because they were weak. We are all the same.

Kancho: Even in the United States, if someone has a dojo and a small, weak, cowardly person comes to train, they should take him in and teach him. These people need to learn all of the good values that karate can instill, and we need to teach them and make them stronger through karate. Even if a seemingly strong person with a good build and lots of courage comes to train, we must then teach this person the true spirit of budo. They must learn that martial arts make the weak person strong and the strong person kind. This is an essential element that many people do not grasp. When I first started karate, in my mind I was only thinking that I wanted to be strong, and nothing else. However, as I continued along the Path, I began to understand the true nature of budo.

Sensei Kishi: People who already think that they are strong do not usually come to practice martial arts. I think that I am the most cowardly person in the world. When I lose, I feel mortified. I hate to lose because I don't want to

Women's demonstration at the 1997 Sabaki Challenge.

feel that way, so I try very hard, both consciously and unconsciously. If I don't practice, I get worried. If humans think that they are strong, they won't try anymore. That's the end. Being self-satisfied is no good. It's only when you think "I'm weak" that you feel you need practice. That's why being old or weak is no excuse to stop practicing; instead, these are the reasons to continue to practice. A lot of people say that they are too old to start karate, but they shouldn't think that way. Any time is a good time to start.

Kancho: Osu. That's true, isn't it?

Sensei Kishi: Everyone has worries and weaknesses. You can feel sorry for yourself, or you can hide from the problems, or you can face the problems head-on and deal with them. Only the last way will make you stronger. To master your problems is very important. Don't hide from them; face them. Suffer through them, become aware of them, and finally overcome them.

Everyone has problems. Life is a journey from one challenge to the next, but those challenges can make us stronger. If you think that you are weak, but constantly push forward, you gradually become stronger. However, the opposite is true as well; if you think that you are strong, you will very possibly become weaker.

Kancho: In the end, the Way of Martial Arts is more about dealing with yourself, not the world. It is a process of building up your own mind and body. Your soul needs to open up and see things in a different light. Some people say that a small man can try very hard, but still never win because he is small, or that an old man will never win because he is too weak; but I don't believe that. Generally speaking, the fact that a person naturally has a big body is mostly luck. A big body is helpful; this is true. A small body is hard to compete with; this is also true. But you can turn that disadvantage into an advantage by seeing it as a challenge that can moti-vate you. Even if you are small, if you try hard, it's still pos-sible to beat a bigger person. That's why training is more about speed, technique, and spirit—not size. You can't give up just because you're at a disadvantage. You can always try to find a way to win.

Sensei Kishi: That's right. Believing that small people will lose and big people will win narrows your possibilities. The person who believes this will not be able to become a good martial artist. In the same sense, if someone becomes older and thinks that they won't be a good karateka because they are old, they have also narrowed their possibilities. Certainly it's difficult to become a good karateka. You must train hard, using different devices and techniques. The late Sensei Kenichi Sawai was an old man, and a very strong *budoka* (true martial artist). But even though he was an old man, when he was fighting I could still feel his strength. His nobility, grace, and grit shone through. This internal strength is the power that you gain from budo.

Kancho: Osu. That's true. I've gone to visit other martial arts schools, and I once heard the story of an old teacher who did a demonstration. The man was ninety years old and had been unable to walk for some time. Two of his students supported him under each arm and brought him to the mat. This old man summoned his strength and power and gave an extraordinary demonstration—not for its technique or power alone, but for his will to perform. The man who told me this story thought that this was a pure example of budo. Just by watching this old man's demonstration of spirit, he had been moved to tears. This is a rare thing to witness; it can inspire and ennoble us.

Sensei Kishi: That's right. The martial arts teachers' job is to show their students how to fight hardships and difficulties, like old age, to teach them that their lives can be strong in every way. To be a good teacher, you don't always have to be stronger than your students. Don't worry that as you get older and weaker no one will come to learn from you. When you get weaker and have difficulty walking, you can use this weakness to show your students how to face this type of challenge. This is just another form of budo. Look at the example of the old sensei who gave his demonstration. Who says that you can't learn anything from an old man? This is not true! I'd prefer to learn from that kind of teacher. As you get older, the Way of Martial Arts, which starts on the outside with technique and basics, gradually progresses to your interior (*shinjitsu*). When your experience begins with fighting and ends in your heart, then it is true budo.

But you can't start off by going straight to the heart. In your youth, it's important to build up your body. Young people have a body that is capable of being built up if they work hard at it. You're foolish if you don't use it. It would be unnatural not to. In the martial arts, inexperienced and incomplete people need to work hard and to be dedicated in order to master themselves. Training is an unfinished circle, a continuous process that never ends. When you are young you have a young body. That's when you need to be thorough in building up your techniques, and you need to fight as often as possible. Instinctually, however, fighting is the human being's biggest fear. One way to look at karate fighting is that it can be cruel. Humanity's hidden brutality is exposed during a fight. Through the process of continuous fighting, however, you can begin to understand not only true human nature, but also your individual nature as a person. When you start to lose your power, you need to constantly invent new ways to compensate. You can't always count on power as you become older; you need to expand your views. It's like the saying: "You can't see the forest for the trees." Don't fixate on the fact that you're getting older. Just use your mind now instead of your body. Some day your body won't be able to move. At that point, look back at the path that you covered to get there, and don't despair. If nothing else, you can still read the *Dojo Kun*. And on that day when your lips no longer move, then it is okay to stop training. On that day, the angels will come down from the heavens and take you home. When that day comes for me, I will happily say goodbye to this life. When I look back, I will see that it was successful. Even this is not quitting. It is more of a graduation from this life to the next.

When he became old, the famous samurai, Musashi Miyamoto, felt that he had to write the *Book of the Five Rings* to pass down to following generations. He said, "Until I was thirty, I continued fighting, undefeated. Perhaps my opponent was weak, or maybe I was naturally gifted. I was over fifty years old before I actually understood strategy. Until then, I was only naturally strong and lucky." The *Five Rings* contains Musashi Miyamoto's life lessons. He was a genius, but even he did not understand these aspects of his fighting until he was older. Even if I train my whole life, I may never have that kind of genius, but then again, maybe I will. That is what training is for. As long as you continue training, there may never be a limit to what you may learn or accomplish.

Each person has his or her own individual path along the way of martial arts. Each individual's body and mind is different. Follow this path to discover your life's purpose. On the way, you may also discover the mystery and wonder that life holds for you. Polish your personality as if it were a precious stone in the rough. If you don't do these things, and just try to better yourself by reading famous people's books—by just looking at the words and not training—that is incomplete. You must experience these things for yourself. You can't just read books, and then say, "Martial arts is technique," or "Martial arts is mind," or "Martial arts is meditation."

Kancho: Reading books alone is no good. You have to sweat, or else you will never understand. You must use your body, not just your mind; you have to polish yourself through real fighting or it will not be authentic. Even though using the mind can help you figure things out, by using your body even more possibilities and solutions will open up to you. Karate is not just in the brain, and not just in the body. It is the combination of body and mind that opens up endless possibilities. You can't separate your shadow from your body, any more than you can separate your mind and body; the mind does not exist without the body. You can't merely think about techniques and expect to perform them; you must train these combinations and movements into the muscles and nerves. This takes effort and sweat . . . thought *and* practice.

Sensei Kishi: For example, when you are young, you have so much power that you can use techniques that actually pick your opponents up off the mat and throw them down. As you get older, you turn to techniques that allow you to take your opponent down using less force. In karate there are two opposing elements; we can call them "light" and "shadow." When the samurai wanted to build up the legs and hips, they used to jump over hemp, a plant that grows incredibly fast. Every day the hemp would be higher than before, and the samurai would have to jump higher and higher. This exercise made the legs and ankles strong. This is an example of the "light" element of training. However, when you get older, instead of jumping up over an obstacle, little by little, you can dig a hole and jump down into it. The impact makes your ankles strong and when you climb up from the hole, it makes your legs strong. This is more of the "shadow" technique. This type of device is very important. Even you, Ninomiya, when you do Sabaki, you use these two elements. You either attack and take people down offensively (light), or react and take them down defensively (shadow).

Kancho: That's true. Younger people who are just looking to win tournaments cannot understand these concepts of "light" and "dark." This idea is only understood once you've dedicated your life to karate.

Sensei Kishi: For young people who are training, tournaments are not necessarily bad, but you should not allow them to become the beginning and end of your training. The ancient kata cannot be taken straight into fighting, but the concepts that you learn from the kata help you in actual fighting. The deep breathing, the strong, unshakable stance, and the strength in your inner being all carry over into your fighting. You can combine both old and new techniques to develop into a strong fighter. But someone who is only thinking about the tournament—about winning and losing—cannot combine the old and the new. They are only thinking about winning, and have not taken the time to integrate the older techniques. Some people are looking for breathing techniques or mental techniques such as those found in meditation. They search them out, but they don't realize that all of these things already exist in karate. You don't need to look outside to find them. It's okay to be lost and looking for different paths, but by training in karate, you can find that it holds everything that you're searching for.

Kancho: Karate can relate to many things in your life. Training for a tournament is like studying for an exam that tests you on your technique and skill; it should be both useful and fun. If you are looking at the tournament as an exam, then your training becomes entirely focused on how you will win the tournament, and not on how karate relates to the other parts of life. If you are a teacher, you must look more widely and deeply, and must not focus on just one aspect of karate. You must teach all kinds of things.

Sensei Kishi: Exams and tournaments are only a small part of life and karate. That's why, when you were twenty-one years old, Ninomiya, and took third place in the World Tournament, I told you, "So what if you didn't win the tournament?" Maybe I was being nosy, but I knew that karate was very broad, and that you had all the time in the world. If you had won that tournament and thought that was everything there was to know, that would have been regrettable, because I knew that the possibilities were endless for you. That's why I told you that, and it was good that you didn't win then.

Kancho: Osu. I remember that. I really think that it was true. When I was twenty years old, Sensei Kishi, I clearly remember you telling what not to do. Even now those words are a treasure to me. Whenever I said, "I'm hungry," or "I'm getting tired," or if we were working outside and I said, "It's hot," you always told me, "Don't say it's hot in the summertime! Of course it's hot! It's summer! Don't say things that are obvious. Samurai don't say obvious things," you would scold. What you said was true.

Sensei Kishi: Yes, you remember that, do you? (laughing) Musashi Miyamoto said, "Think deeply about life and society, but don't think too deeply about yourself." Even in karate, you need to think deeply. There are only a few basic techniques in karate. A lot of people watch karate and think that they can master the moves, but if you are just watching it from the outside, you can actually only see about a third of what karate is. Just like in an old-style Japanese garden, where they traditionally place a large stone in the garden, only about a third of the stone is visible above ground. The rest is buried, rooted in the earth, and it is this that gives the stone its foundation and strength. In karate, what you see on the surface are only the movements, the basics. It is the two thirds that are buried that are so important. Yes, you can master the basics, but you can't just ignore the rest. This is very important. It is when you have mastered the basics that you become *shodan*.

I have a friend, a judo teacher, who trains world-class fighters. His name is Sensei Matsumura. When he looks at a picture of a karate practitioner, even if he can only see his upper body in the photo, he can tell whether or not the person's lower body is grounded. Even though he can't see the "roots," anyone who is a true martial artist—if they have that foundation in themselves—can see it in others.

Kancho: Yes that's right. Enshin Karate's different techniques and variations are shown frequently in magazines now, particularly in Japan. People see the pictures and think that's all there is to it, but there is more than what meets the eye. The training of the mind and spirit is not always apparent in the pictures you see in magazines. This only comes through in doing karate.

Sensei Kishi: That's true. Even techniques come from a combination of both basics and spirit. For example, when an ember is spit from the fire and lands on your hand unexpectedly, you automatically think, "Ow!" That's true for anyone, even a martial artist. The sense of shock and surprise can cause a normal person to lose his composure. But a martial artist can reach inside, ground himself, and deal with it without showing outward distress.

Ninomiya, when you were fighting in the All-Japan, your fighting was magnificent. Since you had mastered the basics before style, you were able, even in the most difficult fights, to use your beautiful, flowing style. It was like watching a master calligraphy artist versus a child printing in block letters. The people fell in love with you, but by watching you, some people tried to imitate the more advanced style without first learning the basics. Because they never took the time to learn the basics, they became frustrated and dropped out. They will never master your style, without learning the basics. Martial arts start from kata (form) and end with kata. By progressing from the basics, you can accomplish anything in martial arts. As I was saying, learn the basics thoroughly. Kishi Karate has the same basics and students do them over and over and over. Eventually what happens is that they develop their own personal style that naturally fits their body type.

Kancho: I agree. In the United States there are some people who try to learn karate today, kung fu tomorrow, and kick boxing the day after. These people occasionally come to my dojo, but I don't believe that their attitude is good. If a student is trying to learn Enshin Karate and another style at the same time, I tell them I don't want them in my dojo. I don't say this because I am small-minded, but because I have put my whole life into Enshin Karate; and I know that other teachers in other styles do the same thing. If you want to learn martial arts, whether it is Enshin Karate or another style, you must put your whole mind into that particular training. You must be committed and dedicated to that style. If you want to truly master the martial arts—just as you said, Sensei Kishi—you must learn the part that is hidden and underground. This is the heart of karate, but it only emerges through practice and hard work. Learning the shape, weight, and size of that foundation, not just the surface—that's what is important. That's why you can't train at the same time in more than one style. I don't like to hear someone say that he's learning Enshin Karate along with other types of karate, because that person is trying to ride two horses at once; he will never master any one style.

Sensei Kishi: That's why when people say, "I can do this style and I know that form, and I also have a black belt in such-and-such," what it really means is that they can't do anything. This is not the meaning behind learning martial arts. In order to learn, you have to dedicate your whole life to understanding the deep foundation. Those people who only take what they see on the surface will never have that foundation themselves.

Kancho: In my dojo I also teach from experiences in my life, passing on my experience to the next generation. I am not selling my technique for tuition, but rather hoping to teach my students, who will then teach their students.

Sensei Kishi: These days, perhaps it's difficult for people to understand these kinds of values, which come from the highest part of budo. A monkey who falls from a tree is still a monkey, but when a martial artist leaves martial arts, he is no longer a martial artist.

What Is Real Karate?

Sensei Kishi: When you read a karate book these days, you begin to think that real karate is just a matter of punching the other person in the face. It doesn't explain that carelessly forming the fist and hitting your opponent's face will break your hand. It doesn't tell you that, although the region around the eyes and brain in the human head is very weak, the bones surrounding them are very strong. If you don't form the fist properly, you'll end up breaking your hand. Just aiming at and hitting the head is not the ultimate jissen (real fighting). Even if you say, "I fight in tournaments in which we allow punching to the face," that is not necessarily real karate.

Kancho: In Enshin Karate we also strive for real karate, but my tournament's rules are geared toward encouraging technique as well. Street fighting, where anything goes, cannot and should not be allowed in a tournament. This is the lowest form of fighting and brings out the worst in all of us. It is raw animalistic combat without technique or spirit. Tournaments should raise us up.

Sensei Kishi: That's right. I don't believe that tournament fighting should ever be the same as real karate on the street.

Kancho: Through practicing karate you better yourself. You build many aspects of yourself: strength and power, as well as character and spirit. Practicing martial arts is never just about survival alone. Your well-being is always important, but so is your opponent's. More people should think this way. "No holds barred" tournaments are spectacles that engage our worst instincts; they appeal to a morbid curiosity. This kind of spectacle does not belong in real karate. In real karate, it is the *doing* and the *practice*—the day-to-day *commitment*—that is important. Even if you put on a real karate tournament, you should not allow any breaking of bodies or breaking down of respect. These kinds of tournaments should not be allowed. It is possible to have a tournament that is close to real karate, but has rules that prohibit punching to the face or kicking to the groin. You can use lots of throwing techniques and sabaki techniques that still allow knockdowns or knockouts. These techniques can be very effective. But finishing off with crippling joint locks, or blows that needlessly injure an opponent just for the pure spectacle, is dangerous and dehumanizing; it should not be permitted. Karate should be positive. You should not be allowed to completely disable or dehumanize your opponent. That's why I developed a point system for the Sabaki Challenge. Once a year my tournament gives fighters a chance to challenge themselves to the limit, but its rules ensure that they respect one another in the process.

Perhaps on the street, in a situation when your life is at stake, you will attack an opponent's vital points or use karate's destructive power to finish off; but these are things that should not be done in the dojo or at a tournament. What is the point of making a tournament that is so dangerous, only a few people would be willing to compete? Karate should be for everyone. These dangerous techniques are not just being found in tournaments, they're being practiced in dojos as well. If you truly know karate and understand the spirit of budo, you will use self-control and not hurt others unnecessarily or cripple them for life, just to show your power.

Sensei Kishi: Like you, Ninomiya. When you fight, you do it with fire, but at the same time you remain cool enough to analyze the situation and do what's appropriate. You never get carried away and needlessly hurt an opponent. That is a wonderful quality. The Way of Martial Arts is serious, and that's why if you're serious about it, you can see beyond the present situation. Even against an opponent in a tournament, you are always aware of his essential humanity. That's what the meaning of natural karate is. Even the tournament itself is only one step on the Path. Tournaments are only a different form of practice.

Kancho: For me, one of the ways of budo is the education of the challenge. Even a tournament is a way to practice and a place to shape yourself. Even in Japan, we are now doing the All- Japan Sabaki Challenge tournament and Sabaki tournaments in Kansai and Shikoku. Small tournaments are held at different schools, and we divide the fighters by weight and belt color. We start with beginner, intermediate, and advanced fighters, who compete regionally and then advance to the Enshin All-Japan in Osaka. For these fighters the tournament experience is not just one isolated event. It is a process. We don't do it for the audience, or to draw large crowds; it is for the fighters to gradually challenge themselves as they move up to the next level. Moving from tournament to tournament, year to year, the important thing is that they continue, not that they reach their goal and then quit. If an Enshin student has enthusiasm and dedication, he or she can even cross the Pacific Ocean and come to the United States.

Sensei Kishi: Just as you did twenty-five years ago, Ninomiya.

Take Your Life into Your Own Hands

Sensei Kishi: These days people's minds are packed with information that they've gotten from books and TV. They don't use their own minds; they just count on the knowledge that they've gotten from others. There is only one truth, but there are many different ways to arrive at it. It depends on your lifestyle and your life experience as to how you reach certain conclusions. Young people think a certain way. They are impatient and only look at the surface of things. They don't understand its roots. Maybe that's why it's hard for many of them to function in society. I think that the problem is not that these young people don't get along with other individuals, or with society as a whole, but that they don't get along with themselves, because they aren't in touch with their own roots. They let what they see on TV and what they study influence how they think and the ideas that they have. They don't see clearly and develop their own point of view.

Kancho: Mmmm. That's right. Osu. What other people think doesn't matter. You need to see a situation clearly and have the courage to make up your own mind.

Sensei Kishi: Imagine a TV set. If you have good antenna, you can see the picture clearly. If you don't, the picture will be fuzzy, unclear. Your personality is the antenna. If it is developed fully, you can live your life clearly, operating on your own feelings and not others. If you have not developed your own personality, you will be confused and the path you are on will be unclear. After I had been training for a long time, I began to personalize my karate for my body and my personality. I began to think that this was the right way. I didn't choose it because it was the easier way, but because it was a complete expression of my personality. Don't put the center of your life in your head. Put it in the center of your being, in your spirit. And if you put your mind into your spirit, then the worries of this world will not affect you. Other people won't unduly influence you. Nothing else will matter.

What Is a Real Champion?

Sensei Kishi: In the world today, so many people call themselves karate teachers or champions of karate. But what makes a true champion is the way he comes back down from the top of the mountain. This is what makes him different. In a karate tournament there is going to be a champion who stands on top, and people will give him praise, and he will praise himself as well. All of this is fine, because you use your own power and heart to climb this mountain path. Once you get to the top, you think, "I did it." You think you've finished, you're through. It's OK. Then you relax and start back down the mountain. You're so happy that you lose the sense of intensity. You're smiling, the body relaxes and maybe you relax too much. You casually go down the mountain, and maybe you let up on your training, and you become fat and lazy. But once a true champion leaves the mat and starts back down the mountain, he never loses his intensity and concentration. He never relaxes as others do. He may have retired from tournament competition, but not from the life of a martial artist. He is still a fearsome person because until the day he dies, he will continue to train.

This type of champion is a true samurai, because he understands everything, but he doesn't need to say it. If anything were to threaten a student, he would try to protect that student and take on the risk himself. He accepts responsibility without casting blame on others.

What Is Sympathy?

Sensei Kishi: Bullies are conceited cowards who are easily influenced. The ones who are getting beaten up are perhaps the stronger individuals. They take the beating and think about how to get back at the bullies. But if you can stop and think about what is happening, then it's also a type of training; then it can make you stronger. Think of it as a positive experience, not a negative one. The real danger is in running away. That will only make them want to punish you more. Stand up and take it, or fight back.

One day in New York, a group of men approached me on the street. One man asked if I had any money. I answered, "Yes, of course I have money." This broke their rhythm. They could sense something from me; and instead of pursuing it, they just looked at each other and left. When the Yakuza come, they have their own rhythm as well. If they are sent to collect money from someone and that person refuses, then they shout, "This is not a child's errand!" My answer to them is, "That's right. You don't look like a kid." This breaks their rhythm. They have a rote way of doing things, but if you break that pattern, they become confused and will often give up. Stand up for yourself and be strong, but also have some ideas as to how to confound your attacker's expectation. In this type of situation, you have to be sympathetic enough to understand your opponent's frame of mind. Then you can move him in another direction. Don't you think so, Ninomiya?

Kancho: I agree. However you choose to confront a threat, you need to do it on your own. This builds up your own mind and spirit. If you worry about getting beaten up and rely on someone else to intervene, you may escape a difficult situation and consider yourself lucky. You may feel relieved to have escaped danger. You feel at peace again, because someone sympathized with your situation and stepped in to take you out of danger. But it shouldn't be that way. You should have peace because you made yourself stronger and were able to change your own situation. This way is more valuable.

Sensei Kishi: For children to understand the importance of self-reliance, we sometimes need to be hard on them. If we want to make them sharp, sometimes we have to be cruel. If I'm driving and a child runs into the road in front of my car, I get angry and sometimes threaten, "I'm going to run you down!" When I go to the mountains, where there are steep cliffs and dangerous drop-offs, and children are carelessly running around, I warn them, "Be careful!" in a very strict and severe way. If you really care about children, smiling and being kind may create a false sense of security when they need to be more aware of real dangers. Sometimes, to be sympathetic, you have to show them tough love.

The Foundation of Karate

Kancho: A dojo has to be a place of learning. Karate teachers need to think more about how they educate their students, because people can learn to think deeply in the dojo. For example, many schools concentrate only on the physical side. If you are studying karate, you are learning potentially deadly skills and you need to learn to control these techniques and weapons in a positive way . . . you need to be an admirable person. As a teacher, you need to set a good example. This is something that becomes evident to students when they watch their sensei. The dojo has to be a place that teaches more than just the physical.

Sensei Kishi: Children who are just starting karate say, "Which is more important? Karate or studying?" Your wife may say, "Which is more important? Karate or me?" and society may say, "Which is more important? Karate or work?" I always hear about cases like this. Through studying karate, you will be a better student, you will be a better husband, and you will be able to work harder. People will say, "Because he is practicing karate, he is different from others." This is how people should view karate. They should see that it gives you the strength and discipline to do well in anything that you try. The dojo is a place that develops people as individuals, and that produces samurai—independent, self-reliant, strong-willed human beings. This is the true origin and purpose of karate . . . to better oneself. I discovered karate over forty years ago, and through karate—by continually being involved and trying hard—I found that I grew as a person. If I didn't have karate, I would have nothing. It is everything to me.

Kancho: I have always respected that about you. Your karate is not only about becoming a stronger fighter, but a better person.

Sensei Kishi: Kinichi Sawai, the martial arts master, liked to encourage his students to be patient and wait for their time to come. He would say, "Even a broken clock is right twice a day." Time itself conforms even to a broken clock; but just like the immobile hands on the clock, you must be strong and shape yourself through martial arts and wait until your time comes. There is nothing new under the sky, but even in dirt, there are still the seeds of kindness and a lovely heart. These seeds are made to flower and grow through the way of martial arts.

What Kind of Talent Is Necessary in Karate?

Sensei Kishi: Ninomiya, why are you doing your open tournament?

Kancho: For students to test themselves. So they can shape the mind, body, and spirit. When you are young, you need to have a goal that keeps your fire burning and motivates you to try hard.

Sensei Kishi: That's right. Why do you do karate?

Kancho: For the same purpose . . . to develop the mind, body, and spirit.

Sensei Kishi: Magazines, videos, and TV show a lot of tournaments. This is supposed to be a place where you develop yourself, but people start to think that if they win these tournaments, they will also be successful in society. They think they will be more influential in their dojo and their organization. Don't misunderstand. The power of budo is not just to be able to speak your mind and be influential. It exists so that we can develop the strength to be able to distinguish right from wrong. To get stronger, you have to make your spirit stronger. The person who trains and competes only so he can have power and influence is a very limited human being. And that is a very sad thing indeed.

Kancho: If you only train and develop your strength to intimidate others, like a lion baring its fangs, that's not true budo. Budo searches for inner strength. What's more important than abusing or hurting your opponent is to conquer the weakness that you find in yourself. That's why budo has something for everyone. People say that a healthy body promotes a healthy spirit, but it doesn't happen automatically. You can't just assume that you will develop a healthy spirit without trying. You have to constantly think about it and work on making it stronger. If you are only putting effort into building your body, strength, and reflexes, you are going down the wrong path; it doesn't matter how hard you try. On the outside, you may look as fierce as a lion baring its fangs, but, on the inside, all you have done is make yourself weaker. You have to constantly be mindful of this.

Sensei Kishi: As Kancho of Enshin Karate, what do you think is required for someone to be a student of Enshin?

Kancho: Two things: a serious mind and perseverance. Yes, natural talent and strength are nice, but what is really important is seriousness. Even if you have perseverance, but are not serious, it's no good. And just being serious isn't enough. You must have the determination to stay on the path, in order to see where it will lead you.

Sensei Kishi: That's true. Ninomiya, we've been around for a long time in the world of martial arts. We've seen so many talented, strong people who have not continued or gone on to be teachers. You cannot be a top martial artist if you're not serious. It doesn't matter how strong you are. Ninomiya, when you were fighting, you were fearsome and strong; but even more than that, you were serious. You had the budo spirit.

Kancho: Osu!

Sensei Kishi: Live straight. That's the most important thing. If your personality is not good, then your karate will never be good. If you really want to do karate, then you first need to change your personality. If you're not making progress in this area, then your karate won't progress either. This is what God gave you. If you have a good personality, your karate will reflect that. This may be a very hard thing to do, but it has great value.

Memories of a Great Spirit

Kancho: Mas Oyama developed full contact karate in Japan. He single-handedly modernized and reshaped karate as no one before. Even though he died in 1994, I still think about him frequently. I came from a branch, and then I moved to the US, so I didn't have a chance to meet with Kancho Mas Oyama much, but Sensei, you were an uchideshi at the headquarters.

Sensei Kishi: But Ninomiya, when Kancho Oyama came to the United States, he still had great affection for you.

Kancho: When Mas Oyama came to the US, he would feel badly, because I had to close the dojo to come see him—he would give me a couple of hundred dollars. When we had the branch leaders' meeting in Hawaii, I would always wear a suit. One time I showed up wearing a suit with sneakers. He stared at my feet for a minute, then said, "Ninomiya, go buy yourself some shoes!" and he gave me some money. I really appreciated his compassion.

Sensei Kishi: He always got really mad at me! Everyone would always say, "Mas Oyama is very friendly," but they didn't know the real Oyama. When he got mad, he got unbelievably mad! If a normal person were to see that, they would tremble in fear. He was not like normal men. To the same extent that he could worry about people and care about them, he could also get angry with them. That big body would turn red, and steam would come out of his ears. That's when people got so scared, and no one wanted to be anywhere near him.

Kancho: I was sixteen years old when I first met him. Sometimes, when I saw him from behind as he was walking, he looked like a walking tatami mat—he was that broad. It wasn't just that he was physically large; he also carried an enormous sense of power. Even from behind, you could sense his presence and his spirit.

Sensei Kishi: That's right. I agree. When I was an uchideshi, I lived in what was called the "Young Lion's Dormitory" and trained with another student, whom I shall call the Teacher's Pet. For some reason, Mas Oyama always got mad at me. When he would call me, I would come running at full speed, to get there as fast as possible. When I arrived I would be out of breath, but didn't want to look bad, so I would stand outside his door and do *shinkokyu* and *ibuki* (exercises to bring the breath under control). Finally, I would say, "Osu!" and go in. Then Oyama would say, "Why are you so relaxed? What took you so long?" When the Teacher's Pet was called, he would run in there out of breath, and Mas Oyama would say, "Thank you!" while smiling. It happened like this all the time, so one time I used a stopwatch to compare how long it actually took for the two of us to get there. My time was actually faster! Another time, all of the uchideshi were called by Mas Oyama. The Teacher's Pet was sleeping with his head on the table, and he came a little late. But when Mas Oyama saw the mark of the desk on his forehead, he said, "You are so enthusiastic! You were training doing head-butts!" and he started laughing. I almost fell over; it was so funny. Then he added, "But if you do too much head-butting, it's not good for your brain. Please be careful."

Kancho: For me, Mas Oyama was a person who was above the clouds. I read a lot of his books, like everyone else. For a lot of young people around the world, he became a hero and inspired their dreams. One of my favorite stories was about how Mas Oyama shaved off one eyebrow after his mentor told him that even a genius has to work incredibly hard to succeed. It inspired me to work even harder to become a good martial artist. I even wrote this saying on the top of my sandbag, and I saw it every day as I trained. If you want to have a dream, you have to work hard. This is what I kept thinking to myself.

Sensei Kishi: Mas Oyama was about thirty years old when he started the Kyokushin style. He would say that he couldn't concentrate on his own training. He said, "I thought I would get strong, but I realize that I'm only half as strong as I wanted to be because I've gotten so busy doing other things." As a karateka, he had a dream that inspired him until the day he died. You could sense it. He was very different from other people in the way he faced difficulty; he was extremely determined. Mas Oyama once called me and said, "Go to Taiwan." He wanted me to establish Kyokushin in that country. So I said, "Osu! I'm going. I'll be back." He said, "Are you stupid?" I was puzzled. He said, "You just said 'you're going, and you'll be back.' You're going there to spread karate, but you'll never know if you'll be coming back. Just say you're going!" I changed my answer and said, "I'm going!" Then, right after that, he said, "Oh, I almost forgot. There's a man there they call the Taiwan Devil. He's over 6'4" tall. Please take care." What that really meant was, "I want you to challenge him, knock him down, and take over Taiwan for Kyokushin." He had that type of resolve, and expected it from his students. If you think that you're going to continue in the way of martial arts, it doesn't matter who is waiting for you, does it?

Kancho: That's true. You need to think about what you need to do from all different angles. Make practice perfection. When you have to do something, do it. Hunker down, take a firm stance. When you no longer worry about living or dying, that's when you're ready to do it.

Sensei Kishi: That's right. I could always see that in you. When I watched you fight, I could always tell by your face that you were ready. At any rate, I went to the Taiwan Devil's dojo and knocked down five of his students; then finally I said to him, "Let's fight." He kept saying he didn't want to! I kept asking and he kept refusing. Later, I called Mas Oyama's headquarters and said, "Ummm, Mas Oyama, I really tried, but the Taiwan Devil doesn't want to fight with me." He said, "Oh? Is that right? Then that's OK." That one word made me so relieved. I had done my job.

When I was young I decided to study Kyokushin Karate. When I was an instructor, Mas Oyama directed me to go to Taiwan, the United States, Romania, and Italy. I went to each country and tried as hard as I could to do what needed to be done. Mas Oyama told me, "Wherever you go, the Japanese have to win. Otherwise, the other countries will never learn. Japan is always seen as a very civil and courteous country. It is also a country of bushido, the samurai spirit. So you must first have this spirit and belief, and then you must spread it to the world and teach others." He felt that for Kyokushin Karate and bushido, if you are going to spread it to others, first you must have a strong belief, as he did. I learned this style from him. I think that if you can learn this kind of strength from the creators of styles, this will only make you stronger.

The Way of Karate—The Way of Man

Sensei Kishi: Real men are happy for other people and cry for other people. To cry for oneself, or to be happy for oneself, is not what a real man does. To cry out of sympathy, that is the mark of a real man. To cry for your own pain is not. Cry for other people's pain, not your own.

Kancho: When I was young and living in the United States, the strength of your spirit helped me many times. You never abandoned anyone when they were going through hard times. You didn't just help with words, but with actions. It didn't matter if you risked yourself or your body. You didn't care. If someone needed your help, you gave it wholeheartedly.

Sensei Kishi: Well, my way of living is not polished. Some people arrive at their destination in a roundabout way, some in a straight line. I go from point to point as needed. If someone that you care about is having a hard time, you can't abandon him. Budo can be a very hard, difficult way; but, at the same time, it can be a very warm, fulfilling way. If you're just interested in becoming famous, or hurting someone, then you're taking a short cut. Sometimes you need to do things in a more circuitous way. You should do things honestly, truthfully, and sincerely. It may take longer, it may be harder, but it's better.

Kancho: Because of your help, I now have this truth inside of me.

Growing with Karate-do

I was not alone in my quest. I started in karate with a group of men, almost all of whom were in their early twenties. It has been a source of strength for us to watch one another grow up in karate, to observe how it has taken on a deeper meaning in our lives, to sense how our spirits have grown.

That is the beauty of karate; like any art, it is ageless. You can grow old with it and never exhaust its dimensions. That is one reason I selected the Japanese character En in Enshin; it stands for a circle that is not quite completed. It symbolizes a journey in karate that is never finished, because for each goal that you achieve, you set another and then another. In this way the mirror will always need polishing, and the ninth degree will never pass himself on to the perfection of tenth. In this way I continue to ask the same question, knowing that no single response will ever fully answer me. In this way I will go on challenging myself, because the sword will always need sharpening.

A televised speech in my hometown of Hizuchi after a demonstration in 1998. A number of American Enshin instructors joined me for the Tenth Enshin Anniversary Summer Camp.

If we were looking only for power, then we wouldn't need to sweat and train. We could simply go out and buy a gun. The purpose of karate is more than building strength. It is to find peace—not merely the peace that comes from settling a fight, but the peace within that shows us our own mind, helps us to understand it, and takes us beyond.

Mirrors

In most dojos there are mirrors so students can watch their technique and improve their form; it is a tool that is helpful at first. After a while, however, you don't need a mirror to tell you if you are doing your technique correctly. You will know by feel if it is right or wrong.

In my dojo, I have students of all ages, from all walks of life: doctors, lawyers, professors, bricklayers, young and old together. At first these students are attracted to karate for different reasons, but in the long run they begin to look for something larger than an effective roundhouse kick or a well-toned body. And the ones who persevere will find it in their own way.

Karate should build not only bodies, but minds, too. This does not mean making that mind larger or being able to fill it with more facts and figures, or even enhancing its memory. Instead it is a process of building an awareness of how the mind works, the channels it follows, and how the mind, in turn, leads the body.

After a period of time these doctors, lawyers, and bricklayers may tell me they find that karate has enhanced other parts of their lives: home, school, work. I am not surprised. The lessons learned in the dojo are easily carried out into the world; karate teaches the lessons of life itself, condensed into a much smaller space.

The dojo is a place for looking at yourself in a very honest way. You may not like the laziness you see or the anger and fear that surface. But these are all direct reflections of what you carry inside. The important thing is to see how these feelings arise and to learn how to move beyond them. So the work in the dojo is done not only on the body itself, but on the mind and heart as well.

You learn very quickly what is useful in the dojo. You learn that anger and fear are not useful in a fighting situation, because they only tighten your muscles and slow your response. That is why it is important to move beyond those emotions. Doing so in your training in the dojo will help you move beyond those emotions in your life outside as well. In this sense the mind is like a mirror. The mirror doesn't lie, but it often shows you only what you are willing to see.

Dojo Kun

The Dojo Kun is a simple code of behavior—a road map showing the way both in the dojo and in life. For those who have made the effort honestly, repeating the Dojo Kun at the end of training is a way of confirming that effort.

"We will always be courteous and show respect to others.

"We will strive to be our best, and pursue it with patience.

"We will develop the mind and body to enhance the spirit.

"We will always keep an open heart and mind.

"We will accept the spirit of challenge.

"We will follow the meaning of Enshin in both our training and our daily lives."

The Polished Sword

There is a well-known story about a very famous swordsman who had lived many years and was approaching the end of his life. He wanted to leave behind for his students a message that would continue to show them the way even after he was gone. For the last time he called his students to his side.

"In my entire life, do you know what my greatest happiness has been . . . my highest achievement?"

The young fighters looked at one another, then jumped up in turn and tried to answer. One praised the master's overwhelming power, another his lightning speed, still another his flawless technique.

"No, none of those," he said, shaking his head.

"My greatest joy," he announced, "is that I have never needed to draw my sword in actual combat."

The students looked at one another, confused, and then the master explained.

"The spirit that I have developed through training," he said, "was like the sharpened edge that results from the care and patience that goes into maintaining a fine sword. My training has made me powerful and quick and nearly perfect in my technique, but it has also built my spirit as well. But to have achieved all of those things without having drawn blood is the greatest achievement of all."

In budo it is not the number of victories that polishes the mind and heart, but the process itself—the *way* that maintains and prepares those skills both internally and externally.

There are many such "ways," and in Japan we call them arts. In addition to the martial arts there are painting, poetry, flower arrangement, pottery, and the tea ceremony. These are all ways to arrive at the same understanding of spirit.

A mountain has only one peak, but many trails lead up to it. Karate is simply one path to the greatest happiness. It can bring strength, understanding, wisdom, and peace. These are the ultimate rewards of a life in karate-do, and I will never stop exploring its ways.

GLOSSARY

banzai (ten thousand years): A wish of everlasting happiness offered on festive occasions.

bokuto: A wooden sword used in the practice of kendo (sword fighting).

budo/bushido: The martial arts and their code of behavior originating in eleventh-century Japan. Influenced strongly by Zen, the precepts of budo (bushido) emphasize the development of character and selfless mental discipline along with fighting technique. Hagakure encapsulated this philosophy by saying, "Bushido means finding how to die."

butsudan: A small shrine in a Japanese home set aside for the remembrance of ancestors.

dojo (way place): A place where the way is learned; an area dedicated to training in a martial art.

doryoku shojin (give your best effort to reach it): An expression used by Buddhist monks to those who have established a goal, as a means of encouraging them along the way.

futon: A bed made of cotton padding with a cotton or cover. Usually rolled up and stored during the day.

gakusei-huku: A student uniform.

ganseki-otoshi: A throwing technique in wrestling similar to a fireman's carry, in which the opponent is grabbed under the arm and inner thigh and thrown onto his back.

geta: Wooden sandals.

gi (clothes): A karate gi is the traditional training uniform.

gunbai: A sumo referee's fan.

hiki kuzushi/hiki mawashi: Grabbing techniques for effecting a powerful transition to the opponent's blind-spot position. Hiki kuzushi: defender grabs the attacker's lead arm by the sleeve and pulls him forward, off balance, setting up a roundhouse kick counterattack. Grabbing the attacker's lead arm and hooking his neck (hiki mawashi) with the opposite hand is used for a close-distance knee kick.

ibuki: Exercise to bring the breath under control.

ipponzeoi: A one-armed shoulder throw in judo.

jissen (real fighting): Because jissen karate is based on principles of real fighting as it would occur in the street, it is said to be more practical. Enshin Karate is based on jissen.

judo: A one-hundred-year-old martial art that uses holding, throwing, choking, and sweeping techniques. It developed from the thousand-year-old art of jujitsu, a specialized form of sword fighting practiced at close range.

kancho (head of an organization): Often the master of a given style of martial art.

karate (empty hand): A martial art developed in the sixteenth century when Chinese sailors taught Okinawan farmers empty-handed techniques to be used for self-defense against marauding soldiers of local warlords. It utilizes punches, kicks, blocks, and some throwing techniques.

karateka: A karate practitioner.

kata (form): In karate, kata refers to a formalized sequence of techniques simulating response to a variety of attacks. Kata is practiced to build technique, speed, power, and spirit.

kendo (sword way): A modern form of the traditional martial art using a shinai, or bamboo sword, instead of a steel blade.

kiai: A loud shout issuing from deep in the belly. It concentrates energy at a point called the seka tanden (one inch below the navel) and focuses effort and concentration.

kohai (one who follows): One with relatively less experience.

kumite: A formalized karate fight or sparring session that takes place in the dojo or at a tournament, as opposed to a scuffle in the street.

makikomi nage: Forward rolling throw.

mawashi geri: A roundhouse kick.

mushin (no mind): A level of extremely deep concentration in which all distractions fall away and the mind is focused on a single point. In a state of mushin, the body performs with a natural and spontaneous correctness of movement. It is a state of consciousness usually attained only after rigorous training.

nidan: Second-degree black belt.

nihon-zuki: Double punch.

nukiuchi: A technique in sword fighting (kendo) in which the swordsman draws his sword and attacks simultaneously.

osu (perseverance): A form of greeting extended from one Zen monk to another to encourage each other along the way. Often used in karate dojos as a sign of greeting, respect, or understanding.

randori: Free practice of attack and defense in judo.

sabaki (redirecting a force to your advantage): A controlled movement out of the line of an opponent's attack into a position of advantage (usually the opponent's blind spot) from which one can counter most effectively.

samurai: The warrior class of swordsmen who usually fought in the service of local Japanese warlords in the period from the eleventh to nineteenth centuries. Samurai were identified by the short and long swords they carried. They were given special privileges and subscribed to the principles of bushido.

san-dan: Third-degree black belt.

sankaku geri (triangle kick): A roundhouse karate kick angled up at forty-five degrees and directed under the opponent's arm to the side of his rib cage.

sankaku jime: A judo choking technique using the legs in a triangular configuration similar to a figure four in wrestling.

seka tanden: The area surrounding a point on the line between the tailbone and navel that is considered the balance point of the body and believed to be the gathering point for physical power.

senpai (one who precedes): One with relatively more experience.

sensei: Teacher.

shiatsu: A form of Japanese massage using finger pressure.

shihan: A teacher of high rank who trains other teachers.

shinai: A bamboo sword used for practicing kendo.

shinkoku: slow breaths to regulate breathing after exercise.

Shinto: Japan's indigenous spiritualism, which identifies the spirit nature, or kami, in all things in the physical world. Its main tenet: "Stay pure and follow the true impulses of your heart."

shoshin (first mind): It refers to the first inspiration that initiated a given effort. To act with shoshin is to perform with the same spirit that inspired you to undertake that action in the first place.

suki: An unguarded moment in which an opponent's concentration or will lapses, creating an opening for attack.

sumo: A form of Japanese wrestling in which the opponents attempt to either push one another out of a ring or throw one another to the ground.

tokkun: Extra training in a given martial art.

tombi: A kite or small bird of prey similar to a hawk.

uchideshi: students who board at the honbu and help with teaching and maintaining the dojo

uchikomi: The practice in judo of "fitting in" for a throwing technique without actually completing the throw.

uchimata: An inner thigh throw in judo.

ushiro geri: A back kick.

yoshi koi: (Ready, come on!)

Ed Zorensky and Kancho Joko Ninomiya

**FOR FURTHER INFORMATION ON ENSHIN KARATE
OR THE SABAKI CHALLENGE, PLEASE WRITE:**

**Kancho Joko Ninomiya; Honbu
4730 E. Colfax Avenue
Denver, Colorado 80220
303-320-7632
www.enshin.com**